Eustace Neville Rolfe, Domenico Monaco

A Complete Guide to the Small Bronzes and Gems

in the Naples Museum according to the new arrangement - reprinted from

The complete handbook. Second Edition

Eustace Neville Rolfe, Domenico Monaco

A Complete Guide to the Small Bronzes and Gems
in the Naples Museum according to the new arrangement - reprinted from The complete handbook. Second Edition

ISBN/EAN: 9783337251475

Printed in Europe, USA, Canada, Australia, Japan

Cover: Foto ©Andreas Hilbeck / pixelio.de

More available books at **www.hansebooks.com**

A COMPLETE GUIDE

TO THE

SMALL BRONZES AND GEMS

IN THE

NAPLES MUSEUM,

ACCORDING TO

THE NEW ARRANGEMENT.

REPRINTED FROM THE COMPLETE HANDBOOK.

THE ORIGINAL WORK BY

DOMENICO MONACO,

CURATOR OF THE MUSEUM;

ENGLISH EDITOR:

E. NEVILLE ROLFE, ESQ., B.A.,

HEACHAM HALL, ENGLAND.

Author of "Pompeii Popular and Practical" and other works.

SECOND EDITION.

TIPOGRAFIA EDITRICE E. PIETROCOLA — NAPOLI

SMALL BRONZES.

This collection of small bronzes numbering some thirteen thousand specimens, nearly all found in Pompeii or Herculaneum, is the unique feature of the Naples Museum.

This department never fails to interest the passing visitor, while it is a mine of wealth to the antiquary, as it contains many perfect specimens of the every day articles of personal use and ornament which eighteen centuries ago were connected with the public and private life of the Roman citizens.

All these articles, from the elaborate Curule chair to the most common kitchen utensil, are designed and executed with an artistic grace which reaches the acme of perfection and elegance. Their number alone is sufficient to stock several museums, and such in the elegance of their form and the perfection of their execution that they are no doubt correctly attributed to Greek artistis, who alone would be likely to carry their taste for ornament into such minute details.

The difference between the work of these Pompeian artists and that of the artificers of our utilitarian age is especially noticeable in this rooms. Everything in a Roman house displayed the master hand of the artist in an unaffected but quite unmistakable manner; whereas our household chattels, being made to a pattern and in vast numbers, though they answer their purpose admirably, may justly be treated as being the production of a mechanical age, testifying rather to the skill of the artisan than to the taste of the artist.

The painting on the walls are of no artistic merit. Is especially notewhorthy the Judgment of Salomon, and exploits of the Farnese family.

" The asterisk (*) denotes the specimens illustrated in Signor Monaco's large work, and the dagger (†) other noteworthy objects.

1

FIRST ROOM.

IN THE CENTRE,

*72983. (*On an antique marble table*). ECONOMIC KITCHENER or BRAZIER, in the shape of a rectangular fortress, with towers at the angles. The embers were laid in the centre, and the fire was surrounded by a jacket of water contained in the conduit beneath the battlements. The water could be drawn off by a tap in one of the sides. Spits for roasting were laid across the embrasures. (*Herculaneum.*)

72984. A rectangular brazier, with four castors. (*P.*)

72985. Bronze bench on five feet. (*Pompeii.*)

*73018. CYLINDRICAL STOVE (*calidarium*), of exquisite beauty. It stands on three lions' feet and has four handles, of which two are fastened to the sides by models of human hands. On the upper part are two handles, each of them formed by two spirited wrestlers. (1863, *Pompeii.*)

THIS STOVE STANDS ON

73019. A round marble table which served as the base of a fountain. The water flowed away through the lions' masks on the edge. (*Herculaneum.*)

109831. Brazier with original ashes in it. (*Pompeii.*)

*72936. (*Upon a modern marble table*). ECONOMIC KITCHENER, consisting of a covered cylindrical boiler, communicating with a hollow semicircle, provided with a tap. The fire within the semicircle heated the boiler, and the three swans upon it are constructed to carry a saucepan. (*Stabiae.*)

†72987. Bronze pedestal of a table formed of a rectangular column, surmounted by a bearded head of Bacchus bearing a cup. In front of the column a charming "Victory," holding a martial trophy in her right hand, rests her feet upon a globe. (*Pompeii.*)

73145. (*On a column.*) Splendid vase with four handles decorated with female busts and richly inlaid with silver. (*Herculaneum.*)

111047. Folding table in bronze, with "*semisanto*" marble top. The edge of this table is inlaid with silver. (*Pompeii.*)

*72988. BISELLIUM with ornamentation in copper. (*P.*)

72989. Brazier damascened in copper. (*Pompeii.*)

73020-1-2. THREE SAFES (*arcae*) all found empty. The centre one, which is of iron, is the finest. Its observe is adorned with bronze nails and two busts of Diana in relief; between them, the head of a wild boar. Beneath, two busts of genii of Bacchus, and the mask of a Bacchante. (*P.*)

IMMEDIATELY BELOW THE THREE SAFES STANDS,

*109983 and 111764. Two PULVINARIA, used by the ancients for the Penates and the sacred vessels at the Lectisternia, important festivals, when the gods were placed at table as if they partook of the sacrifice. (*Pompeii.*)

†78673. Two-handled ewer of very remarkable construction, supported on three Sphinxes with lions' claws, and intended for heating water. (*Pompeii.*)

THIS EWER STAND ON,

78613. A small round table. The three legs represent greyhounds jumping up. (*Pompeii.*)

*72990. LAVER for lustral water. (*Pompeii.*)

72991. BRAZIER. The observe and reverse are adorned with Genii, head of Medusa, and two lion's masks. (*P.*)

72992. BISELLIUM adorned with the heads of asses. (*P.*)

72993. Small tripod с 1 lions' claws for sacrifices. (*Herc.*)

72994. FOLDING TABLE. These legs have acanthus leaves on the upper parts, from which young satyrs are ermerging, each one holding a rabbit under his arm. (*Pompeii.*)

73115. (*On a column*). Ewer, the handle of which represents a winged figure standing on a Cupid who clasps a swan. Very fine. (*Pompeii.*)

*72995. (*Under glass, on a Pompeian mosaic table*). SACRIFICIAL TRIPOD, of exquisite execution adorned with beautiful arabesques and bearded heads of Jupiter Ammon. The legs are braced together by elegant sprays of lotus flowers. The basin is adorned with festoons and the skulls of bulls. (*Herculaneum.*)

72997. Double iron ring used as stocks. Lock missing. (*P.*)

*72998. STOCKS found in the barracks at Pompeii. Four skeletons were found in this terrible instrument, the suddenness of the calamity not permitting of their release. (*P.*)

†109697. (*On a round marble table*). BRONZE VASE, on a quadrangular base. This vase is one of the finest in the collection, and especially remarkable for its handles. (*P.*)

†111050. SMALL CHAIR WITH BACK; the only specimen of its kind. The woodwork is modern. (1876, *Pompeii.*)

*73000. (*Under glass, on a Pompeian mosaic table*). CANDELABRUM formed of a decorated Corinthian column. Four branches issue from the top of the column, from which double-wick lamps hang by four-stranded chains. Upon the left angle of the base, which is inlaid in silver, we observe a fine group of Acratus (a genius of Bacchus) mounted on a panther, the *rhyton* in his hand, and opposite to him a small altar, upon which burns the sacred fire. (*House of Diomede, Pompeii.*)

73144. A very fine ewer found in a Greek tomb. (*Locri.*)

73003 and 73007. The baths, the only bronze ones yet discovered. (*Pompeii.*)

†73005. GREAT BRAZIER found in the *tepidarium* of the baths near the Temple of Fortune at Pompeii.

BEHIND THE BRAZIER,

73017. Four-legged bench from the public baths. (*P.*)

Six CANDELABRA, adapted to a single lamp. They are telescopic, and constructed to take to pieces in a very ingenious and simple manner. (*Pompeii.*)

Sundry circular braziers ornamented with reliefs. (*Pompeii* and *Herculaneum.*)

73146. (*On a column*). A very fine bronze vase, the handles of which represent a combat of gladiators. (*H.*)

73016. IRON STOVE covered with *lapilli*. It has places for two saucepans, and the bottom is of fire-brick. (*Pompeii.*)

Surrounding the room,

A large number of candelabra, or lamp-stands. (*P.* and *H.*)

On the top of the wall-cases,

Sundry kettles and amphoræ. (*Pompeii* and *Herc.*)

Wall-case No. I., (to the left on entering),

68763 *et seq.* Bronze baskets of very elegant form. (*P.*)

Wall-case N. II.,

68808 *et seq.* Ten garden stools. (*Pompeii* and *Herc.*)
68823 *et seq.* Small pans, with spouts and nozzles. (*P.*)
68843 te 47. Five flattened globular water-bottles, of the same shape as European soldier use now. (*Pompeii.*)

Wall-case No. III.,

*68851. Pails (*hydriae*). These water-buckets are richly inlaid with arabesques and animals in silver and copper. Observe especially nos. 68854, and 68866. (*P.* and *H.*)

Wall-case No. IV.,

68935 *et seq.* Jugs similar to those now used for oil. (*P.*)

Wall-case No. V.,

A large number of Jugs, with three lips, and one handle, of highly artistic form. Observe Nos. 69044 to 69048. These jugs were for table use. (*Pompeii* and *Herculaneum.*)

Below,

Twelve *praefericula*, with single lip and handle. (*P.*)
*69087. Libation cup, of very beautiful execution. The edge is surmounted by an eagle with its wings spread out. The handle is formed by a swan. (*Nocera.*)

Outside, on a column, under glass,

†69089. Libation cup of oblong shape. This is quite a unique specimen. (*Ruvo.*)

Wall-case No. VI.,

Several Milk-jug with one handle. Observe those called

"*a petto d' oca* " — that is, "*goose-breasted;* " especially.
(*Pompeii* and *Herculaneum.*)

†69174. LIBATION CUP (*rhyton*), representing the ,head of a stag with silver eyes. The mouth, being, partly open, allowed the liquid to flow out. Examples of the use of this vessel may be seen in the frescoes downstairs. (*Herc.*)

WALL-CASE No. VII,

Observe Nos. 69317 to 69322, and 69318. A JUG, ornamented with two griffins resting their claws upon_an urn. (*Pompeii.*)

WALL-CASES Nos. VIII. TO XI. (SECOND CORNER OF THE ROOM),

Large number of vases, which, to judge by the ornaments on their handles, were used for household purposes. The handles are specially beautiful, and an endless variety of elegant form is displayed in their construction. (*P.* and *H.*)

WALL-CASES Nos. XII, TO XIV.,

Two-handled ewers for household purposes. (*P.* and *H.*)
69725 *et seq.* CINERARY URNS, made of lead. (*Pompeii.*)

FOUNTAIN JETS AND SPRAYS.

WALL-CASES Nos. XV, AND XVI. (THIRD CORNER OF THE ROOM),

69762 *et seq.* Ten tiger heads for fountains. (*Herc.*)

69784-9. A PEACOCK with spreading tail; a column capped with three dolphins; a pine-cone; a serpent; a cylindrical and a conical vase with jets, all forming a group for a fountain. These specimens are set up on wood to show their exact position as found. (1853, *Pompeii.*)

69799 *et seq.* Thirty-two taps and a lead pipe. (*Pompeii.*)

79838 *et seq.* Four gratings made of perforated lead for gutters, and several oblong pans. (*Pompeii.*)

IN FRONT OF THE WINDOW,

*73153. CURULE CHAIR (*sella curulis*), made to fold. Its four crossed legs are fastened by two nails with large heads. (*Herculaneum.*)

FIRST TABLE-CASE No. XXVIII.,

One hundred and forty-three vase handles, finely executed and adorned with heads and arabesques.

72582-3. Two serpentine handles, each serpent holding a cockchafer in his mouth.

†72592. Very fine handle, representing a Phrygian with a pair of shoes on, and his feet crossed. (*Pompeii.*)

†72600. SUPERB HANDLE, the gem of the collection, adorned with arabesques and inlaid in silver, with head of Medusa. (*Herculaneum.*)

72637. HANDLE. Apollo holding the lyre and the *plectrum.* Below, a swan with spreading wings. (*Pompeii.*)

NEXT TABLE-CASE No. XXIX.,

72722-3. Two legs of a table, with lions' claws, each representing an armless Sphinx issuing from three leaves. (*P.*)

72727 *et seq.* Four legs of a table, with greyhound claws. (*Pompeii.*)

BATHING REQUISITES.

WALL-CASE No. XVII.,

*STRIGILS (*strigilis*), used by the ancients after gymnastic exercises and vapour baths to scrape off the perspiration and the ointments. (*Pompeii* and *Herculaneum.*)

69904. Complete apparatus for Roman bath, consisting, of an opening ring upon which are strung four strigils, one *patera*, and one ointment-pot. Observe n.° 115732. (*P.*)

Sundry small pots (*guttus* or *unguentarium*) in bronze or alabaster, for containing perfumed ointments. (*P.* and *H.*)

LOCKS AND KEYS.

WALL-CASES Nos. XVIII TO XX.,

70981 *et seq.* Long borders inlaid with silver, serving as horizontals for bedsteads. (*Pompeii.*)

*LOCKS in bronze and iron. Some have keys. (*P.* and *Herculaneum.*)

Sundry keys of all sizes, some of which are very complicated. (*Pompeii* and *Herculaneum*.)

71283 *et seq.* Padlocks, very curious. (*Pompeii*.)

*71401. IRON KEY, carefully made and inlaid with silver.
It was found upon one of skeletons of the family of *Diomede*, in the cellar of his house at Pompeii.

71392 *et seq.* Bolts of locks. Sundry hinges. (*P.* and *H.*)

BELOW,

71629 and 71630. Two large hinges from one of the city
gates of Pompeii.

TABLE-CASE NO. XXX.,

Ornaments for doors and furniture, including tragic and
comic masks and busts; heads of lions, horses, and other
animals, with movable rings in their mouths. (*P.* and *H.*)

TABLE-CASE NO. XXXI.,

72898 *et seq.* HANDLES for vases, formed of dolphins,
foliage and human hands —STATUETTES serving as handles
for vases. (*Pompeii* and *Herculaneum*.)

†72966-7. Four KNOCKERS with movable ring. These
represent in bas-relief superb heads of Medusa with silver
eyes and teeth. (1870, *Pompeii*.)

†72981. Vase handle with winged Genii in bas-relief,
having their heads pillowed on their entwined arms, and
(on the sides) two Tritons with cuirasses in a striking attitude. In Etruscan style. Duplicate in the British Museum.
(*Borgia Collection*.)

IN FRONT OF THE WINDOW,

†73152. CURULE CHAIR (*sella curulis*), made to fold, with
remains of gilding still discernible. It was originally mounted in ivory, which has been replaced by wood. (*Pompeii*.)

IRON TOOLS.

WALL-CASE NO. XXI., (LAST CORNER OF THE ROOM),

71700 *et seq.* Scythes, sickles, bill-hooks, knives. Rakes

and forks four ploughshares, spades as used in Naples now, and trowels for gardening. (*Pompeii* and *Herculaneum.*)

71746. Small pocket-knife with bone handle. (*Pompeii.*)

WALL-CASE No. XXII.,

71791 *et seq.* Carding combs, long shovel, large spring shears: shears of this form still used in silk factories. Sundry smaller shears, blacksmiths' cutters and pincers, axes, hatchets, soldering iron, claws for drawing nails, pickaxes, wedges, and hammers for chipping pavements. (*P.* and *H.*)

WALL-CASE No. XXIII.,

Hammers for carpenters and masons.—†71875. KEY for raising heavy blocks of stone (as used now), compasses : callipers, masons' trowels, turnery tools, centre-bits, scalpels, planes, saws, anvils, a large whetstone. (*Pompeii.*)

LAMPS AND LANTERNS.

WALL-CASE No. XXIV.,

†72180. TREBLE-WICK LAMP, fitted with three exquisite double-stranded chains; a fourth chain holds the lid of the reservoir. This lamp is adorned with four heads issuing from garlands. (*Herculaneum.*)

72172. SINGLE LAMP. A small mouse on the spout is about to gnaw the wick. (*Pompeii.*)

72181. LARGE TREBLE-WICK LAMP. Instead of a cover it has a handsome urn over the reservoir. This lamp is adorned with festoons and three masks. (*Pompeii.*)

Sundry small candelabra for single lamps. (*P.* and *H.*)

Seventeen lanterns. Observe especially :

*72067. LANTERN glazed with talc, bearing on the top the words "Tiburti Catus S." (*Herculaneum.*)

WALL-CASE No. XXV.,

72190. CANDELABRUM in the form of a cup. (*Herc.*)

72191. CANDELABRUM formed of a fluted column. (*Stabiae.*)

92192-3. CANDELABRA, like modern candlesticks. (*P.*)

72195. CANDELABRUM formed of a fluted column capped by a small vase, from which issue three branches. (*Herc.*)

72246 and 72250. Treble-wick lamps hanging by a well-wrought chain, and decorated with a nude dancer. (*P.*)

72251. Double lamp with garland and sunflower handle. The cover represents a child with a goose. (*Herc.*)

WALL-CASE No. XXVI.,

72198. TREBLE-WICK CIRCULAR LAMP. The lid, which also form a handle, is surmounted by the figure of a Harpy.

72199. SILENUS. His movement and the gestures of his hands leads us to infer that he proposes to dance. Behind him, a parrot on a bough which carries two lamps. (*H.*)

72202-3. PHRYGIAN figure on one knee. Behind him, the stump of a tree with a lamp upon it. (*Pompeii.*)

†72206. LAMP-STAND. Silenus, seated, pouring wine from a wineskin. Behind him, a stum to carry two lamps. (*P.*)

72279. DOUBLE-WICK LAMP. The lid represents a Satyr seated on a stump, holding a pan-pipe. (*Pompeii.*)

72280. Double-wick lamp beautifully adorned with acanthus leaves. The lid bears a Silenus standing upright. (*P.*)

†72291. Handsome small CANDELABRUM. It represents Cupid astride on a dolphin, which is about to devour a polypus issuing from a shell. A wonderful work of art. (*P.*)

†72298. NIGHT-LIGHT in a saucer. The lid is perforated to subdue the light. (*Stabiae.*)

WALL-CASE No. XXVII.,

72226. CANDELABRUM in the form of the trunk of a tree. (*Pompeii.*)

72231. CANDELABRUM in the form of a tree, the boughs supporting five double-wick lamps. (*Herculaneum.*)

†72336. PORTABLE LAMP with folding handle. (*Stabiae.*)

SECOND ROOM.

In the centre of this room is a cork model of the excavation of Pompeii, on the scale of 1 to 100. It is extremely accurate, and well worthy of attention.

The wooden balustrade represents the outline of the ancient ramparts, while the part painted green shows what yet remains to be excavated.

The amphitheatre, which was capable of holding 12,800 people, was situated at the extremity of the town as shown on the model.

The extent of the city is estimated at about one hundred and forty acres, and the part excavated may be taken at about fifty acres, leaving ninety acres still buried beneath a mass of volcanic ash about twenty feet deep, which has been cultivated and even built upon for centuries. The lenght of the excavated portion is about six hundred yards, and the circuit of the city two miles.

The House of Diomede and the Street of the Tombs being outside the walls, are not represented on the model.

AGAINST THE BALUSTRADE OF THE MODEL,

Twelve circular leaden tanks for the *impluvia* of houses, found in the courtyards. One of them has a bronze tap. (*P.*)

SAUCEPANS, PATERÆ, &c.

ON THE LEFT, WALL-CASES NOS. XXXII. AND XXXIII.,

SAUCEPANS, of which many are lined with *silver*. (*P.*)

73231. A SAUCEPAN as found at Herculaneum, completely full of lava and encrusted with ash.

WALL-CASES NOS. XXXIV. AND XXV.,

73437 *et seq.* PATERÆ (or bowls for containing libations). They are of the shape of a deep saucer, with a handle ending in the head of a ram or a swan. (*Pompeii* and *Herc.*)

WALL-CASE NO. XXXVI. (*among a number of two-handled basins*),

73511. BASIN with bas-relief inlaid with silver representing Æthra showing her son Theseus the sword that his father Ægeus had hidden under a rock. (*Herculaneum.*)

WALL-CASE NO. XXXVII, AND XXXVIII.,

73535. BASIN. Two figures in bas-relief one dancing. (*H.*)

BELOW,

73549. BASIN on a tripod with ornate border. The handles are lions, and the sides bear four serpents. (*Pompeii.*)

WALL-CASES No. XXXIX. TO XLIII.,

73613. BASIN with a bas-relief of a woman fashioning a trophy, and Hercules with his club standing by. (*Herc.*)

WALL-CASE No. XLIV.,

73837. Saucepan with long handle covered with *lapilli.* (*P.*) 73798 *et seq.* LADLES used for dipping into vases. (*P.*)

BELOW,

78936. TRAY like a modern tea-tray, but made of bronze. (*Stabiae.*)

WALL-CASE No. XLV. (SECOND CORNER OF THE ROOM),

73838–73863. Twenty-six funnels. (*Pompeii* and *Herc.*) 73879-81-82. Three round stoves. (*Pompeii.*) *73880. URN (*authepsa*). with two handles and lions' feet. This beautiful urn is decorated with designs, and is similar to the Russian *samovar* and the old-fashioned English tea-urn. (*Pompeii.*)

111048. Another elegant urn on three lions' feet, and ornamented with three female masks. The tap represents Cupid astride on a dolphin. (1876, *Pompeii.*)

BELOW,

73886 *et seq.* Stands for vases. (*Pompeii* and *Herc.*) *73937. BRONZE COLLAR for slaves, bearing the inscription : " Servus sum, tene quia fugio." (*I am a slave; arrest me because I am running away*).

73926 *et seq.* SPIRAL GAUNTLETS in bronze, which gladiators wore as a protection for their wrists and ankles.

ARTICLES USED IN SACRIFICES.

WALL-CASE No. XLVI.,

73945 *et seq.* Four portable altars on three legs, suppor-

ting a disc which received the blood of victims. (*Pompeii.*)
†74021-2-3. FLESH-HOOKS (*harpago*) for taking boiled
meat out of the caldron. They were fitted with wooden
handles. There are four similar specimens in the British
Museum. (*Canino.*)
73983 *et seq.* Censers (*turibula*), with chains and spoons
for incense. (*Pompeii* and *Herculaneum.*)

BELOW,
74003 *et seq. Mensae* for the Augurs' (*haruspices*). They
are in the shape of a stool. Upon them lie the instruments
which were used to examine the entrails of the victims for
the purposes of pretended prophecy. (*Pompeii.*)
Bronze letters from inscriptions. (*Pompeii* and *Herc.*)

COUCHES.

IN THE CENTRE,
*78614. Five couches. Two have heads to them. The
wooden part painted red is a restoration; the original wood
was walnut. (*Vibius's house of Pompeii.*)

WEIGHTS AND MEASURES.

WALL-CASE No. XLVII. (*Upper division*),
Eighteen STEELYARDS and SCALES, complete.
74039. The sixth scale from the visitor's left bears the
inscription (in dotted lines): "TI. CLAUD. CÆS. ÆIIII. VITEL.
III. COS. EXACTA, III. TIC. CURA. ÆDIL.;" meaning that this
balance was stamped at the Capitol in the reign of the
Emperor Claudius. (*Pompeii.*)

WALL-CASE No. IL.,
†74056. Under the hook from which this specimen hangs
we read the inscription, "IMP. VESP. AUG. IIX. T. IMP. AUG.
F. VI. COS. EXACTA. IN CAPITO(*lio*);" that is to say, that it
was stamped in the Capitol under the eighth consulate of
the Emperor Vespasian, and under the sixth of Titus, which
corresponds to A.D. 77, two years only before the destruction
of Pompeii. (*Stabiae.*)

74165. Ingenious machine for -weighing liquids. It is in the form of a saucepan, and was suspended by the hook and chain.

LOWER DIVISION *(left),*

Sundry round weights in black basalt (*nefritica*); marked in Roman figures.

74280 to 74290. Eleven round weights in bronze, marked with silver numerals, X, V, III, II, I, S or "*Semis*" (half), for the pounds, and :: ∴ : · S for fractions of pounds.

74308 to 74313. Six bronze WEIGHTS, in the shape of goats. These are marked P.X, P.V, P.III, P.II, P.I.

*74390 to 74393. Four large weights; a PIG, bearing the initials P.C (one hundred pounds); a CHEESE, and two huge KNUCKLE-BONES. (*Pompeii.*)

*Leaden weights, bearing the word "EME" on one side, and "HABEBIS" on the other—"*Buy, and you shall have.*" (*Pompeii.*)

. 74582 *et seq.* Measures for oil. (*Pompeii.*)

74599. Measure for liquids, of the weight of ten pounds.— The *Congius* spoken of by Pliny. (*Borgia.*)

*74600-1. Dry MEASURES. Their capacity was settled by the triangular crosspieces. Inscription: "D. D. P. P. HERC." (*Pompeii.*)

OUTSIDE THE WALL-CASE,

74602. Dry measure. (The wood is a restoration.)   (*P.*)

WALL-CASES NOS. L. AND LI.,

Sundry kitchen utensils. (*Pompeii* and *Herculaneum.*)

MATHEMATICAL INSTRUMENTS.

TABLE-CASE NO. LXI.,

*76657 to 76667. Plummets. (*Pompeii* and *Herculaneum.*)

*76670 *et seq.* Sundry pairs of compasses. (*P.* and *Herc.*)

*76684 Reducing compass. (*Pompeii.*)

†115630. CALLIPERS. This handsome specimen is exactly like the instrument used by modern sculptors. (1887, *P.*)

76689. Square. (*Pompeii.*)

*76690 *et seq.* Linear measures. (*Pompeii.*)

FISHING TACKLE.

76840 *et seq.* Netting needles. bronze and bone needles, quadruple fish-hook weighted.-Four hundred fish-hooks. (*P.*)

109703. A RUDDER, belonging probably to a bronze statue of " Abundance." (*Pompeii.*)

111845. Small iron ANCHOR; the only one yet found. (*P.*)

MUSICAL INSTRUMENTS.

TABLE-CASE No. LXII.,

*76945 *et seq.* SISTRA—jingling bronze rattles used in the worship of Isis. (*Pompeii.*)

*76942. CYMBALS of two kinds (Psalm. cl. 5). (*Pompeii.*)

111055. A bronze wind instrument, like an organ. It was fitted with a chain, apparently to be carried round the neck. (*Pompeii.*)

*76890. BAGPIPES found in the baaracks. The " dulcimer" of Dan. iii. 5. Nero was fond of this instrument, and is said to have played it in public. It is the favourite instrument of the S. Italian peasantry. (*Pompeii.*)

*76891 *et seq.* FLAGEOLETS made of silver, bronze, and ivory. (*Pompeii.*)

TOYS, DICE, AND TICKTES FOR THEATRES.

TABLE-CASE No. LXIII.,

*76950 *et seq.* Knucklebones and. dice; some constructed that they might be loaded. (*Pompeii.*)

*77087 *et seq.* Sundry checks or tickets (*tesserae*) for theatres and boxing matches, made of ivory. Observe the small numbered birds made of terra-cotta. These were checks for the upper row of seats, still called the " *piccionaia* " or pigeon-loft, in Italy. (*P.* and *Herculaneum.*)

109880. Six nnmbered death's-heads (use unknown). (*P.*)

TOILET REQUISITES.

TABLE-CASE No. LXIII. *(bis)*,

77147 *et seq.* Bronze clasps (*fibulae*). (*P.* and *Herc.*)

77170. Fibula in the form of a horse.

114430. Bronze ring with the finger-bone of his owner.

77259 *et seq.* Bronze rings fitted with a small hey for jewel-cases. (*Pompeii.*)

77245. Sundry rings in bone and lead, bearing initials. (*Pompeii.*)

77174 *et seq.* Bronze bracelets,. in the form of serpents, one with a silver medallion. (1863, *Pompeii.*)

*77213 *et seq.* Five perfect metal MIRRORS. One in a modern frame was found in the House of the Faun. (*P.*)

77291 *et seq.* These specimens have long been supposed to be perforated boxes for perfumes, made on the principle of the modern "*vinaigrette*"; but, in fact, they are cases for seals to be attached to parchments. The box contained the seal, and two or more threads of silk attached to the wax passed from the parchment through the holes. One of them may be seen represented upon the large fresco from the House of Pansa attached to the papyrus (see No.8598.p.2).

77298. Small rectangular bolts in ivory, for securing dressing-cases or small articles of furniture. (*Pompeii.*)

77318 *et seq.* Bone buttons and bronze studs. (*P.*)

77355 *et seq.* Ivory and bronze combs. (*Pompeii.*)

77363. BRONZE THIMBLE. (*Pompeii.*)

Small pots for cosmetics. (*Pompeii.*)

*77570. Pot of rock-crystal, still containing *rouge*. (*P.*)

Small flagons in alabaster and ivory, for perfumes. (*P.*)

SPINDLE, fitted with a bronze hook. (*Pompeii.*)

77518. Bronze winder, in nine divisions, for threads of different colour. (*Pompeii.*)

80088. Small toothed wheel, used as part of a bolt. (*P.*)

We draw attention to this little specimen to show how nearly the Romans had reached one of the leading principles of the modern clock.

Hairpins in bone and bronze, adorned with statuettes and busts; tooth-picks and earpickers. (*Pompeii* and *Herc.*)

WALL-CASES Nos. LII. AND LIII.,
Kitchen pots and pans. (*Pompeii* and *Herculaneum.*)

COLANDERS.

CASE LXIV., IN FRONT OF THE WINDOW.
Colanders perforated in graceful designs. (*P.* and *Herc.*)
77609. In the centre of this specimen a bas-relief of Venus with silver bracelets, holding out her hand to a small Cupid. (*Herculaneum.*)

NEAR THE BALUSTRADE OF THE MODEL OF POMPEII,
78579. Large CALDRON, nailed and bolted as our modern steam boilers. (*Pompeii.*)
78580. Large FIRE-PLUG, found in the palace of Tiberius at Capri. The rust of ages has sealed it hermetically.
This specimen once had water in it, which one could hear by shaking it. This has now completely evaporated.

78581. Bronze grating (*claustrum*), found before a window in Pompeii.

SURGICAL INSTRUMENTS (*Chirurgia.*)

TABLE-CASE LXV.,
Bistouries (surgical knives), spatulæ, sounds, and tweezers, some of which last belonged to lamps.
77738 *et seq.* "Directors."
77982. Curved dentated forceps, for removing foreign substances from cavities.

TABLE CASE LXVI.,
77986 *et seq* Fourteen bronze cupping vessels of modern shape, but ours are now made of glass.
78000-1. Spoons with head of a ram and of a woman.
78003. Lancet for bleeding.
78004. Silver spoon with elegant handle.
78005. Scissors with a spring, like shears.
78007. FLEAM for bleeding horses.

2

78008. TROCHAR for tapping for dropsy. A hole in the end gives an exit to the water.

78012. An ELEVATOR (or instrument for raising depressed portions of the skull) made of bronze.

*78026. A MALE CATHETER (aenea fistula).

*78027. A FEMALE CATHETER, 3 1/2 inches in length.

*78029. POMPEIAN FORCEPS, formed of two branches crossing, and working on a pivot. It was used for crushing small calculi.

*78030. SPECULUM UTERI. It is a tri-valvular dilator; the three valves, standing at right angles to the rest of the instrument, are jointly dependent on each other in the expansion transmitted only to one of them. When the three valves are in contact, the instrument for insertion is about an inch in circumference. By turning the screw, one valve is drawn nearer to the operator, and this forces the other two to open in a sidelong direction, producing thus a slow. regular, progressive dilatation, as extensive as may be required. The instrument can be held by the two curved handles in the left, while the right hand turns the screw. These movable handles are similar to those fitted to modern specula. (Pompeii.)

113264. SPECULUM UTERI. A quadrivalvular dilator of beautiful workmanship and very scientific costruction. (P.)

*78031. SPECULUM ANI. A bi-valvular dilator, probably used also for the uterus before the other one was known.

78032. Dentated forceps of elegant construction.

78121. Sound with flattened extremity, bifurcated for cutting the frenum of the tongue ; as used in modern surgery.

78034 et seq. Actual cauteries.

*78071. Surgical needle.

78137. Probes found in the cases to the left of them.

78195-6. Stones for sharpening instruments. (Stabiae.)

*78235. An INJECTION PROBE for females, with eight small holes arranged like wreaths.

*PILLS, SULPHUR, and other medicaments. (Stabiae.)

MORE SURGICAL INSTRUMENTS.

TABLE-CASE LXVI (*bis*),

On the 31.st of October 1887 the following items were found in a house at Pompeii which appears to have been the residence of a Medical man.

116437 *et seq.* Sundry forceps.

116460. Earthenware gallipot containing drugs, the nature of which is unknown.

116460 (*bis*). Plate with similar contents.

116438 Chemist's scales.

116439 *et seq.* Four square bronze weights. These have dots upon them to denote their value — no. 116443 weighs 14 grammes. Besides them are three weights of black stone (*nefritica*).

110088. Small bronze medicine spoon.

116459. Stone for instruments.

116456. Rusty scalpel.

116458. Iron spring scissors.

116450. Large bronze surgical needle.

116435. Uterine dilator similar to that in the preceding table-case.

116436. Anal dilator.

116451. Injecting probes.

116447. Bistouries.

116444. Bronze instrument case still containing its original instruments. — Sundry empty cases.

116441-2. Two inkstands in good preservation.

116453. The hinges and lock of the box which contained the above specimens.

IVORY ARTICLES (*Miscellaneous.*)

TABLE-CASES NOS. LXVII, LXVIII.,

78362 *et seq.* Fragments of furniture made of iron cased in ivory. — Ivory fragments from dressing-cases. — Bone spoons. (*Pompeii.*)

110924. Statuette of Venus with dolphin. (*Pompeii.*)

78279. Statuette of boy wearing the "*bulla patricia.*" (*Pompeii.*)

78306. Fragments from the Curule chair. (*Pompeii.*)

109905 and -5 (*bis*). Two ivory panels (frame modern), carved on both sides, used as ornaments for furniture. (*P.*)

78288. Small bronze skeleton. (*Pompeii.*)

78289. Fine ivory death's-head.

In the window,

The skull and the right fore-arm are so small that they seem to have belonged to a young girl, who was probably a member of the family of Diomede at Pompeii. One of her teeth will be observed in perfect preservation. The various blocks of ashes collected in this case had surrounded the body, and still show the imprint of the breast, of the hands and fingers, as well as of the feet.

WRITING MATERIALS.

Wall-case No. LVI.,

Inkstands, pens, metal mirrors, serpentine bracelets. (*P.*)

75080. Inkstand still containing ink, *atramentum.* (*P.*)

†75091. Octagonal inkstand (found in a tomb at Terlizzi) of bronze, decorated in silver, with the seven divinities who presided over the seven days of the week,—namely, Apollo, Diana, Mars, Mercury, Jupiter, Venus and Saturn.

> Martorelli, the archæologist (who wrote two volumes about this inkstand), thinks that it belonged to some astronomer of the time of Trajan.

110672. Bronze pen, nibbed like a modern one. (*P.*)

In a tube of modern glass,

75095. Pen of reed, found in a papyrus at Herculaneum,

75099. Slabs of stone, which were covered with wax for writing upon with the "*stylus.*"

75113. Two bone "*styli.*" Pointed at one end and flat at the other, to rub out what one had written. (*Pompeii.*)

80111. BRACELET on the bone of a right arm. (*P.*)
75114. Bronze squares from the front of a strong box.

SADDLERY.

WALL-CASE (NEXT THE DOOR) LVII.,

CATTLE BELLS, HARNESS, &c. Large number of bells for cattle. By pulling a wire in the side of this case, one of these bells is made to ring. (*Pompeii* and *Herculaneum.*)

74578. Small model of a BIGA, of very great interest, as showing us the form of Pompeian vehicles. (*Pompeii.*)

HARNESS FOR HORSES, consisting of scrolls, sprays, bits, nosebands, pole-heads, curb-chains, spurs, a stirrup (?), buckles, and other objects which can be readily identified.

75537. A fragment representing a blacksmith in the act of paring a hoof.

KITCHEN UTENSILS.

WALL-CASE LVIII,

PASTRY MOULDS in the shape of shells. (*P.* and *H.*)

76352 *et seq.* Four SHAPES, representing a hare, a pig, a ham, and half a fowl. (*Pompeii.*)

76336. IMPLEMENTS for making pastry.—Pastry cutters.

76349. Cheese-graters.—Bronze kinives and spoons. (*P.*)

WALL-CASE LIX,

76543. Large EGG FRAME, capable of cooking twenty-nine eggs at once. (*Inn, Pompeii.*)

76540-1. Very handsome andirons (?).

Tart dishes, frying-pans, gridirons, tongs, artistic fire-shovels, kitchen trivets. An iron trivet, much oxidised and covered with *lapilli*, with a pot firmly stuck to it by the oxidisation. — Seven spits.

Hanging up against the wall near the door,

78622. A bronze BELL, shaped like a gong. (*Pompeii.*)

It has a beautiful tone, which may be heard by swinging the clapper which hangs before it.

THE COLLECTION OF GEMS.

(Oggetti preziosi.)

This collection has recently been scientifically arranged, and is divided into four principal sections, namely,—Gold Ornaments, Silver Plate, Engraved Gems, and Cameos.

The gold ornaments are very varied, and many of them are of extremely beautiful design. Some of them were found in Greek tombs in the South Italian provinces, but the majority are of the Roman period, and were discovered in the excavations at Pompeii.

The collection of Silver Plate is perhaps the most important extant, and shows a wonderful excellence of design and execution.

CAMEOS AND INTAGLIOS.

This collection consists of about a thousand specimens, many of which bear the name of Lorenzo de' Medici, and came from the Farnese collection. The ancient specimens are marked *"Ant.."* (Antique) and the mediæval ones *"xv."* (fifteenth century).

TAZZA FARNESE.

IN THE WINDOW,

*27611. CUP OF ORIENTAL SARDONYX of inestimable merit and value, found either in the Castle of *Sant' Angelo* at Rome, or in Hadrian's villa at Tivoli. It came into the possession of Duke Charles of Bourbon when he was besieging Rome, and was already disfigured by a hole in the centre, which had been bored through it with the view, no doubt, of fixing it on a stand. It is the only known cameo of its size which has a composition engraved on both sides of it. On the outer side is a magnificent Medusa, and on the inner eight figures in relief representing Ptolemy Philadelphus consecrating the harvest festival instituted by Alexander the Great after the foundation of Alexandria. (*Ant.*)

FIRST TABLE.—FIRST COMPARTMENT (*next window.*)
·25833 to 25899. (*Note especially.*)

1. *Onyx.* THE EDUCATION OF BACCHUS. The infant god, mounted on a lion led by a nymph, is held up by one of the *Nysiades*; behind, *Nysa* seated. *Ant.*

5. *Onyx.* .NEPTUNE and PALLAS disputing about the name to be given to a rising city. Inscribed IY—probably meaning *Pyrgotele.* *Ant.*

*6. *Onyx.* DÆDALUS and ICARUS. Two females admiring the prodigy—probably Pasiphae and Diana Dictyna—personifying the Cretan City. XV.

8. *Oriental Onyx.* TRIUMPH of BACCHUS and SILENUS. The car is drawn by two Psyches, the reins held by Cupid, while another pushes the car. *Ant.*

*16. *Onyx.* JUPITER overwhelming the Titans. Legend, ΑΘΗΝΙΩΝ. *Ant.*

17. *Onyx.* COCK-FIGHT, in presence of two Cupids, one lamenting his defeat, the other victorious. *Ant.*

19. *Sardonyx.* HEAD of OMPHALE. *Ant.*

25. *Sardonyx.* HOMER; name on the mantle. *Ant.*

*30. *Agate.* JUPITER SERAPIS, in high-relief. *Ant.*

*32. *Agate.* Head of MEDUSA. *Ant.*

38. *Agate.* OTHRYADES dying. *Ant.*

†41. *Sardonyx.* SATYR dancing. A fragment. *Ant.*

†44. *Sardonyx.* AUGUSTUS. Attributed to *Dioscorides.*

†47. *Onyx.* AURORA in her chariot. *Ant.*

*48. *Oriental Onyx.* A FAUN carrying the infant Bacchus.

52. *Onyx.* A fine head, perhaps CICERO. *Ant.*

55. *Oriental Onyx.* VENUS and CUPID.

†57. *Sardonyx.* CENTAUR. *Ant.*

*60. *Oriental Onyx.* SCULPTOR chisselling a vase. *Ant.*
*65. *Agate.* DIRCE'S PUNISHMENT. Fragment.
1857. *Onyx enammelled.* VESTAL , a superb head. *Ant·*

SECOND COMPARTMENT.

25900 to 26042.

69. *Agate.* Ariobarzanus III.,. king of Cappadocia (?). *Ant.*
77. *Sardonyx.* DOMITIAN. Laurel crowned. XV.
86. *Onyx.* HERCULES strangling the serpents. *Ant.*
90. *Sapphire.* Veiled head of LIVIA. XV.
93. *Emerald.* Lotus-crowned head of ISIS. *Ant.*
99. *Lapis-lazuli.* Tiberius crowned with laurel. XV.
105. *Emerald.* Bust of JUPITER SERAPIS. *Ant.*
123. *Jacinth.* CLEOPATRA. XV.
124. *Onyx.* MARSYAS bound and MERCURY. *Ant.*
134. *Onyx.* Leda and the swan. *Ant.*
147. *Sardonyx.* HERCULES and the lion. XV.
154. *Onyx.* GANYMEDE AND THE EAGLE. XV.
167. *Garnet.* SAMSON, with legend. XV.
171. *Agate.* DOMITIAN. XV.
†188. *Sardonyx.* AURORA on a *quadriga.* *Ant.*

The artist adapted the different strata of the stone to give
each horse a distinct colour. According to Winckelmann,
their colours indicate dawn, day, twilight, and night.

193. *Onyx.* CUPID; legend—ΦΙΛΩ, *I love.* *Ant.*
· 197. *Onyx.* Hand pulling an ear; ΜΝΗΜΟΝΕΥΕ, *remember.*
Ant.
198. *Onyx.* Hand-in-hand, ΟΜΟΝΟΙΑ—*concord.* *Ant.*
201. *Onyx.* GANYMEDE borne by the eagle. *Ant.*
†203. *Agate.* THETIS on a dolphin , with Triton and
Zephyr. XV.
206. *Glass.* Tiberius. (*Pompeii.*)

INTAGLIOS.

SECOND TABLE — FIRST COMPARTMENT.
26043 to 26209.

*209. *Carnelian.* AJAX and Cassandra at the Palladium. *A.*
†214. *Chrysolite.* PALLAS. XV.
†215. *Chalcedony.* ANTONINUS PIUS (?). XV.
221. *Carnelian.* SOLON. Legend,—ΣΟΛΩΝΟΣ. *Ant.*
228. *Amethyst.* IOLE ; a fine head. XV.
230. *Sapphire.* Fine bust of JUNO. *Ant.*
231. *Carnelian.* Head of MARCUS AURELIUS. *Ant.*
*232. *Amethyst.* DIANA with ΑΠΟΛΛΩΝΙΟΣ inscribed in Greek. A gem of great celebrity. *Ant.*
†234. *Calcedony.* ACTOR with a mask. XV.
244. *Beryl.* Head of SERGIUS GALBA. XV.
248. *Carnelian.* THE CAR OF THE SUN. *Ant.*
250. *Amethyst.* ANTONINUS PIUS. *Ant.*
253. *Amethyst.* THETIS on two sea-horses. *Ant.*
254. *Carnelian.* PERSEUS with Medusa's head. Inscribed "*Dioscorides.*" *Ant.*
256. *Carnelian.* HADRIAN, crowned. *Ant.*
268. *Carnelian.* Fine head of PLATO. XV.
276. *Carnelian.* JULIUS CÆSAR. XV.
287. *Garnet.* Bust of CLEOPATRA. *Ant.*
Carnelian. (The *first* stone from the left, without a number). Handsome bust of JUNO. (*Pompeii.*)
329. *Sardonyx.* MARS crowned by Victory. *Ant.*

SECOND COMPARTMENT.
26210 to 26389.

†390. *Carnelian.* SACRIFICE. Group of 18 figures. XV.
408. *Carnelian.* SILENUS upon an ass. Group. XV.
413. *Carnelian.* PESCENNIUS. Inscribed "*Pescennio*". XV.
417. *Sanguine Jasper.* SACRIFICE. XV.
419. *Carnelian.* LIVIA and TIBERIUS. Group. XV.
439. *Carnelian.* Strength conquered by Beauty.

455. *Sardonyx.* CUPID dedicating one wing to the Sun. xv.
473. *Chalcedony.* AFRICA PERSONIFIED. Engraved with unintelligible characters. *Ant.*

OTHER INTAGLIOS AND CAMEOS.

THIRD TABLE—FIRST COMPARTMENT.
26390 to 26766.

Intaglios of less importance.

SECOND COMPARTMENT.
26767 to 26965.
(CAMEOS).

961. *Agate.* MINERVA, fully armed. Bust. xv.
967. *Onyx.* AURORA in her chariot. *Ant.*
988. *Onyx.* THE THREE GRACES. xv.
1003. *Onyx.* MINERVA. xv.
†1021. *Lapis-lazuli.* MINERVA armed. xv.
†1024. *Onyx.* ALEXANDER THE GREAT. xv.
1044. *Onyx.* MÆCENAS (?). xv.
1046. *Agate.* SOCRATES. xv.

FOURTH TABLE—FIRST COMPARTMENT.
26966 to 27123.

1162. *Agate.* Head of Cicero, KI-KE-PO. *Ant.*
A necklace of scarabs.

SECOND COMPARTMENT.
27124 to 27348.

1375. *Green Jasp.* Aurora. xv.
†1352. A *bulla* mounted with gold wire, representing a man and his wife. Some think that this a portrait of Marcus Aurelius and Faustina. *Ant.*

FIFTH TABLE.
27349 to 27610.

Many portraits in intaglio.

1520. *Sardonyx*. Jupiter. Bust. XV.

1540. *Sea-shell*. Three Cupids drawing water. XV.

1701 *et seq. Agates*. Perfume vases. *Ant.*

Agate. A knuckle-bone. *Ant.*

Large silver-gilt rings belonging to Cardinal Farnese. Some similar rings are exhibited in the Musee Cluny at Paris.

LAST TABLE.

One hundred and forty intaglios and stone all from recent excavations at Pompeii. Observe especially the numbers 27651,-27665,-27653,-14565,-14566,-27617,-114562, and in the last row a beautiful glass intaglio (n.° 109579) representing a Minerva standing.

SILVER.

In an upright glass case :

CUPS AND VASES.

TOP SHELF,

25289. Silver PAIL with bronze handle decorated with a bas-relief of a lady at her bath. (*Herculaneum*.)

25376-77-80-81. Four BACCHIC Cups executed in magnificent high—relief, representing Centaurs and Genii. (*P*.)

15367. CUP representing in bas-relief Minerva in a chariot drawn by two horses. (*Pompeii*.)

25565. Fragment of a cup representing chariots driven by children. (*Herculaneum*.)

25301. Mortar representing the Apotheosis of Homer. One of the most famous specimens of ancient silver work. In the centre is the poet draped and veiled, borne heavenwards by an eagle. On the right a female figure representing the Odyssey. On the left is the Iliad personified armed cap-à-pic. (*Herculaneum*.)

25681. CUP adorned with Bacchic figures.

111149. MORTAR adorned with bas-relief representing

Theseus fighti ng against one of the Amazones on horseback (*Pompeii.*)

SECOND SHELF,

25284-5-8. Three BOWLS on tripod stands of Renaissance work. (*Rome.*)

25343. CENSER with cover and chains. (*Herculaneum.*)

3571o. Two SYSTRA. A musical instrument. (*Pompeii.*)

25722 and 110841. Two BOTTLES for liquids: one with chains. (*Pompeii.*)

THIRD SHELF,

25601 *el seq.* Six pitchers. (*Pompeii and Herculaneum.*)

111768-9. Two large pitchers with two handles. Each weighs about 10 lbs. (*Herculaneum.*)

GOLD ORNAMENTS.

(*Greek and Etruscan.*)

FIRST DIVISION *(on the left)*,

†25234 *et seq.* A pair of very large earrings of pyramidal shape.—A ring, with an agate intaglio representing an Amazon and a small gold coin of Syracuse representing a portrait of a woman. (Gift of Baron d'Arbou Castillon 1864 found in a tomb at Taranto).

24852. GOLD BULL with Phœnician and Greek inscription. (*Syracuse.*)

24826. KID in massive gold from Edessa in Mesopotamia. (*Borgia Collection.*)

24876-8. Two perfume vases in blue glass mounted on a gold stand. (*Venosa.*)

Ten necklaces. The following are the most remarkable:—

*24883. Splendid necklace formed of twenty-one Silenus masks and fifty-eight acorns and *fleurs-de-lys.* (*Armento.*)

*24858. NECKLACE OF LACE-WORK, with elegantly woven pendants.

42.9 27Necklace consisting of seven gold parallelograms.

24862. Necklace with blue beads threaded upon it, to which are attached nineteen masks of Jove, Medusa, and Silenus. (*Chiusi.*)

24887. Necklace of a gold chain with garnets. In the centre a small octagonal column of garnet. (*Sant'Agata dei Goti.*)

BETWEEN THE NECKLACES,

24893. GOLD TIARA formed of a curved spray with leaves and flowers set with garnets, and small gold butterflies. (*Fasano.*)

24854-5-6. Three specimens of beautiful workmanship representing cornucopiae with lions' heads. These are thought to have been earrings. (*Capua.*)

Below them, a pair of earrings in the shape of butterflies.

Among fourteen rings, observe a ring 25157 set with an emerald plasma which is thought to have contained poison. (*Ruvo.*)

24844. Fillet, with a head of Medusa, in relief. (*Toro.*)

*24865 *et seq.* NINE BROOCHES (*fibulae*), artistically wrought in filagree, ending in the head of a ram in Etruscan Style.

(*Roman Period.*).

25000. LARGE GOLD LAMP, weighing nearly two pounds, and having its handle formed of a leaf. It is the only gold lamp yet found in Pompeii. (Grammes 896).

EARRINGS.

SECOND WALL (*first and second divisions*),

*Two hundred and fifty two gold earrings, of which hundred and two are in the shape of a segment of an apple, and many are drops with a pearl as a pendant; seventeen represent genii, two are of the shape of almonds, and others are set with emeralds. (*Pompeii* and *Herculaneum*.)

RINGS.

Three hundred and twenty-three gold rings, most of them set with fine stones.

The first five rows consist of rings from Pompeii, and the last two rows of rings from Herculaneum.—Note;

†In the second row a ring 25181 bearing a mask engraved on carnelian, which was found at Pompeii by King Charles III, who wore it for many years. When this King inherited the throne of Spain, he handed over the ring to the Museum.

24732-3-4. Three rings with the finger-bones of their owners. (*Pompeii.*)

The *provenance* of the rings in the next compartment is unknown, with a few unimportant exceptions which came from the Campanian provinces.

Among them will be found—

A very large ring of unusual shape, with fragment of glazing. Thought to have been a perfume ring. (*Herc.*)

24902. Gold ring. Man and woman shaking hands. Probably an engagement ring. (*Ponza*).

25085. Very large head of Brutus engraved on gold, grammes 3,50. (*S. Maria di Capua*). Inscribed "ΑΝΑΞΙΛΑΣ ΕΠΟΕΙ".

The last row consists of rings of the fifteenth century. Note high-relief of woman in onyx.

NECKLACES.

THIRD DIVISION,

Thirty-two necklaces. Note especially;

111114. Two vine-leaf necklaces, one of forty-eight and the other of forty-six leaves. (*Pompeii.*)

†113576. REMARKABLE NECKLACE of ribbon wire set with eight large pearls and nine emeralds. At one end of it is a gold disc set with an emerald, at the other end is a hook. This is one of the richest necklaces of antiquity. (Length 345 millimetres). (*Found near Pompeii*, 1884).

24650. BULLÆ PATRICIÆ. These trinkets were worn round the necks of patrician boys in Roman times, and were dedicated to the gods when the boys arrived at man's estate. They were called "*bullæ*" (bubbles) from their shape, and are represented on the statues of boys of noble birth. (*Herculaneum.*)

25260. LONG GOLD CHAIN, beautifully worked. This chain was found, together with several of the gold ornaments already described, on the first floor of a house at Pompeii, where eleven persons (whose skeletons were found) had taken refuge. (Length, 2 3/4 yards).

24845-6. Two handsome brooches, to which two gold pomegranates have been suspended.

24857. LION and SPHINX brooch. (*Herculaneum.*)

25222-3. In the flat case are two remarkable buttons with seated female figures in red enamel. (*Pompeii.*)

BRACELETS.

FOURTH DIVISION,

Eighty-one bracelets of various kinds.

*24825. Two large serpeatine bracelets, weighing two pounds (the largest yet found). (*House of the Faun, P.*)

109587. BRACELET of gold wire twisted into figures of 8. (*Pompeii.*)

*24842. BRACELET of two cornucopiæ with lions' heads. (*Herculaneum.*)

The flat portion of this case contains some gold leaf, a purse made of gold network, lady's hair-net of gold wire in perfect preservation, fillets in gold braid.

ROCK CRYSTAL, AMBER.

FIFTH DIVISION,

Many fragments of rock crystal representing insects, cups, a spoon, &c. Several agate scent bottles. (*Pompeii.*)

†27613. A CIRCULAR PIECE OF GLASS, usually called a magnifying lens. This unique specimen has given rise to much discussion. (*Pompeii.*)

Several fragments of amber, among them a small statuette

(25813) of a man wearing a wig, and wrapped in a mantle. (*Pompeii.*)

The rest of the amber was found at *Ruvo*.

25810. A cock and a parrot in mother-of-pearl.

OTHERS OBJECTS IN SILVER.

LEFT CORNER,—WALL-CASE, NEAR THE WINDOW,

A box containing fragments of silver from furniture decorations; much oxydised and mingled with lapilli. (*P.*)

Silver crescent, tweezers and clasps. (*Pompeii.*)

Bracelets, brooches, rings, necklace, and two strigils hung on a ring.

RIGHT CORNER,—WALL-CASE, NEAR THE WINDOW,

Many cups with saucers, in very good preservation. (*P.*)

NEXT WALL,

25695. Silver trays, one oblong, the others round. (*H.*)

WALL-CASE BEYOND THE DOOR *(hanging from top shelf)*,

25494. BRONZE SUN-DIAL faced with silver, in the shape of a ham. The hours are indicated by radiating lines, across which run irregular horizontal lines. Below these are the names of the months. The tail served as a gnomon. (*Herculaneum.*)

25496. Beneath the dial two delicate silver colanders are suspended. (*Herculaneum.*)

CUPS.

Twenty eight cups, among which, two chased cups.

25372. Handsome vase with spiral ornament surmounted with the head of a woman with her hair dressed in modern style.

Pastry-mould in the shape of a shell.

Spoons of various shapes. (*Pompeii* and *Herculaneum.*)

Small spoons with pointed ends, which are thought to have served as forks. (*Pompeii* and *Herculaneum.*)

Sixteen saucepans, the handles engraved with designs.
Sauce-ladles. (*Pompeii* and *Herculaneum.*)

Last wall-case *(top shelf)*,

Several cups adorned with exquisite foliage. Observe;
*25287. Bacchic cup, worked in bas-relief of ivy.
25300. Mortar-shaped cup adorned with beautiful leaves
and sprays. (*Pompeii.*)
25495. Satyr seated on a rock playing the lyre before a
hermes. (*Herculaneum.*)
109688. Diminutive skeleton very well executed. (*P.*)
†25490. The death of Cleopatra. A very fine bas-
relief on the reverse of a circular mirror. (*Herculaneum.*)
25489. Abundance. Circular *plaque*, of perfect preservation. (*Pompeii.*)
109331. Male figure seated beneath a tree. (*Herc.*)
25492-3. Diana and Apollo. Two medallions in high-
relief.
25699. A man and a woman conversing. Silver inlaid
on copper. (*Herculaneum.*)
25482-3. Two arms well moulded, belonging probably to
a statuette.
25497-8. Two hairpins, one representing Venus and Cupid;
the other Venus and Adonis. (*Pompeii.*)

MR. D. MONACO'S PUBLICATIONS.

The following Works may be purchased direct from Mr. MONACO, 21, Via Arena Sanità Naples, and at by F. Furchheim, English and German Bookseller, 59, Piazza dei Martiri Palazzo Partanna, Naples.

SPECIMENS from the NAPLES MUSEUM.
168 Copperplates, with Full Descriptive Letterpress, in English or French. Price 35 francs.

A SMALLER EDITION, containing Plates of the Principal Objects selected from the larger work, Price 30 francs.

A COMPLETE HANDBOOK to the NAPLES MUSEUM, in English and French. Price 5 francs.

ONE DAY IN THE NAPLES MUSEUM Price 2 1/2 francs.

GUIDE GÉNÈRAL DU MUSÉE NATIONAL DE NAPLES. Price 5 francs.

A COMPLETE GUIDE

TO THE

SMALL BRONZES AND GEMS

IN THE

NAPLES MUSEUM,

ACCORDING TO

THE NEW ARRANGEMENT.

REPRINTED FROM THE COMPLETE HANDBOOK.

THE ORIGINAL WORK BY

DOMENICO MONACO,

CURATOR OF THE MUSEUM;

ENGLISH EDITOR:

E. NEVILLE ROLFE, ESQ., B.A.,

HEACHAM HALL, ENGLAND.

Author of "Pompeii Popular and Practical" and other works

SECOND EDITION.

NAPLES

1889.

Price One Franc

A COMPLETE GUIDE

TO THE

SMALL BRONZES AND GEMS

IN THE

NAPLES MUSEUM,

ACCORDING TO

THE NEW ARRANGEMENT.

REPRINTED FROM THE COMPLETE HANDBOOK.

THE ORIGINAL WORK BY

DOMENICO MONACO,

CURATOR OF THE MUSEUM;

ENGLISH EDITOR:

E. NEVILLE ROLFE, ESQ., B.A.,

HEACHAM HALL, ENGLAND.

Author of "Pompeii Popular and Practical" and other works.

SECOND EDITION.

NAPLES

1889.

TIPOGRAFIA EDITRICE E. PIETROCOLA — NAPOLI

SMALL BRONZES.

This collection of small bronzes numbering some thirteen thousand specimens, nearly all found in Pompeii or Herculaneum, is the unique feature of the Naples Museum. This department never fails to interest the passing visitor, while it is a mine of wealth to the antiquary, as it contains many perfect specimens of the every day articles of personal use and ornament which eighteen centuries ago were connected with the public and private life of the Roman citizens. All these articles, from the elaborate Curule chair to the most common kitchen utensil, are designed and executed with an artistic grace which reaches the acme of perfection and elegance. Their number alone is sufficient to stock several museums, and such in the elegance of their form and the perfection of their execution that they are no doubt correctly attributed to Greek artistis, who alone would be likely to carry their taste for ornament into such minute details.

The difference between the work of these Pompeian artists and that of the artificers of our utilitarian age is especially noticeable in this rooms. Everything in a Roman house displayed the master hand of the artist in an unaffected but quite unmistakable manner; whereas our household chattels, being made to a pattern and in vast numbers, though they answer their purpose admirably, may justly be treated as being the production of a mechanical age, testifying rather to the skill of the artisan than to the taste of the artist.

The painting on the walls are of no artistic merit. Is especially notewhorthy the Judgment of Salomon, and exploits of the Farnese family.

" The asterisk (*) denotes the specimens illustrated in Signor Monaco's large work, and the dagger (+) other noteworthy objects.

FIRST ROOM.

In the centre,

*72983. (*On an antique marble table*). Economic Kitchener or Brazier, in the shape of a rectangular fortress, with towers at the angles. The embers were laid in the centre, and the fire was surrounded by a jacket of water contained in the conduit beneath the battlements. The water could be drawn off by a tap in one of the sides. Spits for roasting were laid across the embrasures. (*Herculaneum.*)

72984. A rectangular brazier, with four castors. (*P.*)

72985. Bronze bench on five feet. (*Pompeii.*)

*73018. Cylindrical stove (*calidarium*), of exquisite beauty. It stands on three lions' feet and has four handles, of which two are fastened to the sides by models of human hands. On the upper part are two handles, each of them formed by two spirited wrestlers. (1863, *Pompeii.*)

This stove stands on

73019. A round marble table which served as the base of a fountain. The water flowed away through the lions' masks on the edge. (*Herculaneum.*)

109831. Brazier with original ashes in it. (*Pompeii.*)

*72986. (*Upon a modern marble table*). Economic Kitchener, consisting of a covered cylindrical boiler, communicating with a hollow semicircle, provided with a tap. The fire within the semicircle heated the boiler, and the three swans upon it are constructed to carry a saucepan. (*Stabiae.*)

†72987. Bronze pedestal of a table formed of a rectangular column, surmounted by a bearded head of Bacchus bearing a cup. In front of the column a charming "Victory," holding a martial trophy in her right hand, rests her feet upon a globe. (*Pompeii.*)

73145. (*On a column.*) Splendid vase with four handles decorated with female busts and richly inlaid with silver. (*Herculaneum.*)

111047. Folding table in bronze, with "*semisanto*" marble top. The edge of this table is inlaid with silver. (*Pompeii.*)

*72988. BISELLIUM with ornamentation in copper. (*P.*)

72989. Brazier damascened in copper. (*Pompeii.*)

73020-1-2. THREE SAFES (*arcae*) all found empty. The centre one, which is of iron, is the finest. Its observe is adorned with bronze nails and two busts of Diana in relief; between them, the head of a wild boar. Beneath, two busts of genii of Bacchus, and the mask of a Bacchante. (*P.*)

IMMEDIATELY BELOW THE THREE SAFES STANDS,

*109983 and 111764. Two PULVINARIA, used by the ancients for the Penates and the sacred vessels at the Lectisternia, important festivals, when the gods were placed at table as if they partook of the sacrifice. (*Pompeii.*)

†78673. Two-handled ewer of very remarkable construction, supported on three Sphinxes with lions' claws, and intended for heating water. (*Pompeii.*)

THIS EWER STAND ON,

78613. A small round table. The three legs represent greyhounds jumping up. (*Pompeii.*)

*72990. LAVER for lustral water. (*Pompeii.*)

72991. BRAZIER. The observe and reverse are adorned with Genii, head of Medusa, and two lion's masks. (*P.*)

72992. BISELLIUM adorned with the heads of asses. (*P.*)

72993. Small tripod on lions' claws for sacrifices. (*Herc.*)

72994. FOLDING TABLE. These legs have acanthus leaves on the upper parts, from which young satyrs are ermerging, each one holding a rabbit under his arm. (*Pompeii.*)

73115. (*On a column*). Ewer, the handle of which represents a winged figure standing on a Cupid who clasps a swan. Very fine. (*Pompeii.*)

*72995. (*Under glass, on a Pompeian mosaic table*). SACRIFICIAL TRIPOD, of exquisite execution adorned with beautiful arabesques and bearded heads of Jupiter Ammon. The legs are braced together by elegant sprays of lotus flowers. The basin is adorned with festoons and the skulls of bulls. (*Herculaneum.*)

72997. Double iron ring used as stocks. Lock missing. (*P.*)

*72998. STOCKS found in the barracks at Pompeii. Four skeletons were found in this terrible instrument, the suddenness of the calamity not permitting of their release. (*P.*)

†109697. (*On a round marble table*). BRONZE VASE, on a quadrangular base. This vase is one of the finest in the collection, and especially remarkable for its handles. (*P.*) ·

†111050. SMALL CHAIR WITH BACK; the only specimen of its kind. The woodwork is modern. (1876, *Pompeii.*)

*73000. (*Under glass, on a Pompeian mosaic table*). CANDELABRUM formed of a decorated Corinthian column. Four branches issue from the top of the column, from which double-wick lamps hang by four-stranded chains. Upon the left angle of the base, which is inlaid in silver, we observe a fine group of Acratus (a genius of Bacchus) mounted on a panther, the *rhyton* in his hand, and opposite to him a small altar, upon which burns the sacred fire. (*House of Diomede, Pompeii.*)

73144. A very fine ewer found in a Greek tomb. (*Locri.*)

73003 and 73007. The baths, the only bronze ones yet discovered. (*Pompeii.*)

†73005. GREAT BRAZIER found in the *tepidarium* of the baths near the Temple of Fortune at Pompeii.

BEHIND THE BRAZIER,

73017. Four-legged bench from the public baths. (*P.*)

Six CANDELABRA, adapted to a single lamp. They are telescopic, and constructed to take to pieces in a very ingenious and simple manner. (*Pompeii.*)

Sundry circular braziers ornamented with reliefs. (*Pompeii and Herculaneum.*)

73146. (*On a column*). A very fine bronze vase, the handles of which represent a combat of gladiators. (*H.*)

73016. IRON STOVE covered with *lapilli*. It has places for two saucepans, and the bottom is of fire-brick. (*Pompeii.*)

SURROUNDING THE ROOM,

A large number of candelabra, or lamp-stands. (*P.* and *H.*)

ON THE TOP OF THE WALL-CASES,

Sundry kettles and amphoræ. (*Pompeii* and *Herc.*)

WALL-CASE No. I., (TO THE LEFT ON ENTERING),

68763 *et seq.* BRONZE BASKETS of very elegant form. (*P.*)

WALL-CASE N. II.,

68808 *et seq.* Ten garden stools. (*Pompeii* and *Herc.*)
68823 *et seq.* Small pans, with spouts and nozzles. (*P.*)
68843 te 47. Five flattened globular water-bottles, of the same shape as European soldier use now. (*Pompeii.*)

WALL-CASE No. III.,

*68851. PAILS (*hydriae*). These water-buckets are richly inlaid with arabesques and animals in silver and copper. Observe especially nos. 68854, and 68866. (*P.* and *H.*)

WALL-CASE No. IV.,

68935 *et seq.* JUGS similar to those now used for oil. (*P.*)

WALL-CASE No. V.,

A large number of JUGS, with three lips, and one handle, of highly artistic form. Observe Nos. 69044 to 69048. These jugs were for table use. (*Pompeii* and *Herculaneum.*)

BELOW,

Twelve *praefericula*, with single lip and handle. (*P.*)
*69087. LIBATION CUP, of very beautiful execution. The edge is surmounted by an eagle with its wings spread out. The handle is formed by a swan. (*Nocera.*)

OUTSIDE, ON A COLUMN, UNDER GLASS,

†69089. Libation cup of oblong shape. This is quite a unique specimen. (*Ruvo.*)

WALL-CASE No. VI.,

Several MILK-JUG with one handle. Observe those called

"*a petto d' oca*" — that is, "*goose-breasted;*" especially. (*Pompeii* and *Herculaneum*.)

†69174. LIBATION CUP (*rhyton*), representing the head of a stag with silver eyes. The mouth, being, partly open, allowed the liquid to flow out. Examples of the use of this vessel may be seen in the frescoes downstairs. (*Herc.*)

WALL-CASE No. VII,

Observe Nos. 69317 to 69322, and 69318. A JUG, ornamented with two griffins resting their claws upon an urn. (*Pompeii.*)

WALL-CASES Nos. VIII. TO XI. (SECOND CORNER OF THE ROOM),

Large number of vases, which, to judge by the ornaments on their handles, were used for household purposes. The handles are specially beautiful, and an endless variety of elegant form is displayed in their construction. (*P.* and *H.*)

WALL-CASES Nos. XII. TO XIV.,

Two-handled ewers for household purposes. (*P.* and *H.*)

69725 *et seq.* CINERARY URNS, made of lead. (*Pompeii.*)

FOUNTAIN JETS AND SPRAYS.

WALL-CASES Nos. XV, AND XVI. (THIRD CORNER OF THE ROOM),

69762 *et seq.* Ten tiger heads for fountains. (*Herc.*)

69784-9. A PEACOCK with spreading tail; a column capped with three dolphins; a pine-cone; a serpent; a cylindrical and a conical vase with jets. all forming a group for a fountain. These specimens are set up on wood to show their exact position as found. (1853, *Pompeii.*)

69799 *et seq.* Thirty-two taps and a lead pipe. (*Pompeii.*)

79838 *et seq.* Four gratings made of perforated lead for gutters, and several oblong pans. (*Pompeii.*)

IN FRONT OF THE WINDOW,

*73153. CURULE CHAIR (*sella curulis*), made to fold. Its four crossed legs are fastened by two nails with large heads. (*Herculaneum.*)

First table-case No. XXVIII.,

One hundred and forty-three vase handles, finely executed and adorned with heads and arabesques.

72582-3. Two serpentine handles, each serpent holding a cockchafer in his mouth.

†72592. Very fine handle, representing a Phrygian with a pair of shoes on, and his feet crossed. (*Pompeii.*)

†72600. Superb handle, the gem of the collection, adorned with arabesques and inlaid in silver, with head of Medusa. (*Herculaneum.*)

72637, Handle. Apollo holding the lyre and the *plectrum.* Below, a swan with spreading wings. (*Pompeii.*)

Next table-case No. XXIX.,

72722-3. Two legs of a table, with lions' claws, each representing an armless Sphinx issuing from three leaves. (*P.*)

72727 *et seq.* Four legs of a table, with greyhound claws. (*Pompeii.*)

BATHING REQUISITES.

Wall-case No. XVII.,

*Strigils (*strigilis*), used by the ancients after gymnastic exercises and vapour baths to scrape off the perspiration and the ointments. (*Pompeii* and *Herculaneum.*)

69004. Complete apparatus for Roman bath, consisting, of an opening ring upon which are strung four strigils, one *patera,* and one ointment-pot. Observe n.° 115732. (*P.*)

Sundry small pots (*guttus* or *unguentarium*) in bronze or alabaster, for containing perfumed ointments. (*P.* and *H.*)

LOCKS AND KEYS.

Wall-cases Nos. XVIII to XX.,

70981 *et seq.* Long borders inlaid with silver, serving as horizontals for bedsteads. (*Pompeii.*)

*Locks in bronze and iron. Some have keys. (*P.* and *Herculaneum.*)

Sundry keys of all sizes, some of which are very complicated. (*Pompeii* and *Herculaneum.*)

71283 *et seq.* Padlocks, very curious. (*Pompeii.*)

*71401. IRON KEY, carefully made and inlaid with silver. It was found upon one of skeletons of the family of *Dio-mede*, in the cellar of his house at Pompeii.

71392 *et seq.* Bolts of locks. Sundry hinges. (*P.* and *H.*)

BELOW,

71629 and 71630. Two large hinges from one of the city gates of Pompeii.

TABLE-CASE No. XXX.,

Ornaments for doors and furniture, including tragic and comic masks and busts; heads of lions, horses, and other animals, with movable rings in their mouths. (*P.* and *H.*)

TABLE-CASE No. XXXI.,

72898 *et seq.* HANDLES for vases, formed of dolphins, foliage and human hands —STATUETTES serving as handles for vases. (*Pompeii* and *Herculaneum.*)

†72966-7. Four KNOCKERS with movable ring. These represent in bas-relief superb heads of Medusa with silver eyes and teeth. (1870, *Pompeii.*)

†72981. Vase handle with winged Genii in bas-relief, having their heads pillowed on their entwined arms, and (on the sides) two Tritons with cuirasses in a striking attitude. In Etruscan style. Duplicate in the British Museum. (*Borgia Collection.*)

IN FRONT OF THE WINDOW,

†73152. CURULE CHAIR (*sella curulis*), made to fold, with remains of gilding still discernible. It was originally mounted in ivory, which has been replaced by wood. (*Pompeii.*)

IRON TOOLS.

WALL-CASE No. XXI., (LAST CORNER OF THE ROOM),

71700 *et seq.* Scythes, sickles. bill-hooks, knives. Rakes

and forks four ploughshares, spades as used in Naples now, and trowels for gardening. (*Pompeii* and *Herculaneum*.) 71746. Small pocket-knife with bone handle. (*Pompeii*.)

WALL-CASE No. XXII.,

71791 *et seq.* Carding combs, long shovel, large spring shears: shears of this form still used in silk factories. Sundry smaller shears, blacksmiths' cutters and pincers, axes, hatchets, soldering iron, claws for drawing nails, pickaxes, wedges, and hammers for chipping pavements. (*P.* and *H.*)

WALL-CASE No. XXIII.,

Hammers for carpenters and masons.—†71875. KEY for raising heavy blocks of stone (as used now), compasses: callipers, masons' trowels, turnery tools, centre-bits, scalpels, planes, saws, anvils, a large whetstone. (*Pompeii*.)

LAMPS AND LANTERNS.

WALL-CASE No. XXIV.,

†72180. TREBLE-WICK LAMP, fitted with three exquisite double-stranded chains; a fourth chain holds the lid of the reservoir. This lamp is adorned with four heads issuing from garlands. (*Herculaneum*.)
72172. SINGLE LAMP. A small mouse on the spout is about to gnaw the wick. (*Pompeii*.)
72181. LARGE TREBLE-WICK LAMP. Instead of a cover it has a handsome urn over the reservoir. This lamp is adorned with festoons and three masks. (*Pompeii*.)
Sundry small candelabra for single lamps. (*P.* and *H.*)
Seventeen lanterns. Observe especially:
*72067. LANTERN glazed with talc, bearing on the top the words "Tiburti Catus S." (*Herculaneum*.)

WALL-CASE No. XXV.,

72190. CANDELABRUM in the form of a cup. (*Herc.*)
72191. CANDELABRUM formed of a fluted column. (*Stabiæ*.)
92192-3. CANDELABRA, like modern candlesticks. (*P.*)'

72195. CANDELABRUM formed of a fluted column capped by a small vase, from which issue three branches. (*Herc.*)

72246 and 72250. Treble-wick lamps hanging by a well-wrought chain, and decorated with a nude dancer. (*P.*)

72251. Double lamp with garland and sunflower handle. The cover represents a child with a goose. (*Herc.*)

WALL-CASE No. XXVI.,

72198. TREBLE-WICK CIRCULAR LAMP. The lid, which also form a handle, is surmounted by the figure of a Harpy.

72199. SILENUS. His movement and the gestures of his hands leads us to infer that he proposes to dance. Behind him, a parrot on a bough which carries two lamps. (*H.*)

72202-3. PHRYGIAN figure on one knee. Behind him, the stump of a tree with a lamp upon it. (*Pompeii.*)

†72206. LAMP-STAND. Silenus, seated, pouring wine from a wineskin. Behind him, a stum to carry two lamps. (*P.*)

72279. DOUBLE-WICK LAMP. The lid represents a Satyr seated on a stump, holding a pan-pipe. (*Pompeii.*)

72280. Double-wick lamp beautifully adorned with acanthus leaves. The lid bears a Silenus standing upright. (*P.*)

†72291. Handsome small CANDELABRUM. It represents Cupid astride on a dolphin, which is about to devour a polypus issuing from a shell. A wonderful work of art. (*P.*)

†72298. NIGHT-LIGHT in a saucer. The lid is perforated to subdue the light. (*Stabiae.*)

WALL-CASE No. XXVII.,

72226. CANDELABRUM in the form of the trunk of a tree. (*Pompeii.*)

72231. CANDELABRUM in the form of a tree, the boughs supporting five double-wick lamps. (*Herculaneum.*)

†72336. PORTABLE LAMP with folding handle. (*Stabiae.*)

SECOND ROOM.

In the centre of this room is a cork model of the excavation of Pompeii, on the scale of 1 to 100. It is extremely accurate, and well worthy of attention.

The wooden balustrade represents the outline of the ancient ramparts, while the part painted green shows what yet remains to be excavated.

The amphitheatre, which was capable of holding 12,800 people, was situated at the extremity of the town as shown on the model.

The extent of the city is estimated at about one hundred and forty acres, and the part excavated may be taken at about fifty acres, leaving ninety acres still buried beneath a mass of volcanic ash about twenty feet deep, which has been cultivated and even built upon for centuries. The lenght of the excavated portion is about six hundred yards, and the circuit of the city two miles.

The House of Diomede and the Street of the Tombs being outside the walls, are not represented on the model.

AGAINST THE BALUSTRADE OF THE MODEL,

Twelve circular leaden tanks for the *impluvia* of houses, found in the courtyards. One of them has a bronze tap. (*P.*)

SAUCEPANS, PATERÆ, &c.

ON THE LEFT, WALL-CASES NOS. XXXII. AND XXXIII.,

SAUCEPANS, of which many are lined with *silver*. (*P.*)

73231. A SAUCEPAN as found at Herculaneum, completely full of lava and encrusted with ash.

WALL-CASES NOS. XXXIV. AND XXV.,

73437 *et seq.* PATERÆ (or bowls for containing libations). They are of the shape of a deep saucer, with a handle ending in the head of a ram or a swan. (*Pompeii* and *Herc.*)

WALL-CASE NO. XXXVI. (*among a number of two-handled basins*),

73511. BASIN with bas-relief inlaid with silver representing Æthra showing her son Theseus the sword that his father Ægeus had hidden under a rock. (*Herculaneum.*)

WALL-CASE NO. XXXVII, AND XXXVIII.,

73535. BASIN. Two figures in bas-relief one dancing. (*H.*)

BELOW,

73549. BASIN on a tripod with ornate border. The handles are lions, and the sides bear four serpents. (*Pompeii.*)

WALL-CASES No. XXXIX. TO XLIII.,

73613. BASIN with a bas-relief of a woman fashioning a trophy, and Hercules with his club standing by. (*Herc.*)

WALL-CASE No. XLIV.,

73837. Saucepan with long handle covered with *lapilli*. (*P.*)
73798 *et seq.* LADLES used for dipping into vases. (*P.*)

BELOW,

78936. TRAY like a modern tea-tray, but made of bronze. (*Stabiae.*)

WALL-CASE No. XLV. (SECOND CORNER OF THE ROOM),

73838–73863. Twenty-six funnels. (*Pompeii and Herc.*)
73879-81–82. Three round stoves. (*Pompeii.*)
*73880. URN (*authepsa*). with two handles and lions' feet. This beautiful urn is decorated with designs, and is similar to the Russian *samovar* and the old-fashioned English tea-urn. (*Pompeii.*)
111048. Another elegant urn on three lions' feet, and ornamented with three female masks. The tap represents Cupid astride on a dolphin. (1876, *Pompeii.*)

BELOW,

73886 *et seq.* Stands for vases. (*Pompeii and Herc.*)
*73937. BRONZE COLLAR for slaves, bearing the inscription : "Servus sum, tene quia fugio." (*I am a slave; arrest me because I am running away*).
73926 *et seq.* SPIRAL GAUNTLETS in bronze, which gladiators wore as a protection for their wrists and ankles.

ARTICLES USED IN SACRIFICES.

WALL-CASE No. XLVI.,

73945 *et seq.* Four portable altars on three legs, suppor-

ting a disc which received the blood of victims. (*Pompeii.*)
†74021-2-3. FLESH-HOOKS (*harpago*) for taking boiled
meat out of the caldron. They were fitted with wooden
handles. There are four similar specimens in the British
Museum. (*Canino.*)

73983 *et seq.* Censers (*turibula*), with chains and spoons
for incense. (*Pompeii and Herculaneum.*)

BELOW,
74003 *et seq.* Mensae for the Augurs' (*haruspices*). They
are in the shape of a stool. Upon them lie the instruments
which were used to examine the entrails of the victims for
the purposes of pretended prophecy. (*Pompeii.*)
Bronze letters from inscriptions. (*Pompeii and Herc.*)

COUCHES.
IN THE CENTRE,
*78614. Five couches. Two have heads to them. The
wooden part painted red is a restoration; the original wood
was walnut. (*Vibius's house of Pompeii.*)

WEIGHTS AND MEASURES.

WALL-CASE No. XLVII. (*Upper division*),
Eighteen STEELYARDS and SCALES, complete.

74039. The sixth scale from the visitor's left bears the
inscription (in dotted lines): "TI. CLAUD. CÆS. ÆIIII. VITEL.
III. COS. EXACTA, III. TIC. CURA. ÆDIL.;" meaning that this
balance was stamped at the Capitol in the reign of the
Emperor Claudius. (*Pompeii.*)

WALL-CASE No. IL.,
†74056. Under the hook from which this specimen hangs
we read the inscription, "IMP. VESP. AUG. IIX. T. IMP. AUG.
F. VI. COS. EXACTA. IN CAPITO(*lio*);" that is to say, that it
was stamped in the Capitol under the eighth consulate of
the Emperor Vespasian, and under the sixth of Titus, which
corresponds to A.D. 77, two years only before the destruction
of Pompeii. (*Stabiae.*)

74165. Ingenious machine for weighing liquids. It is in the form of a saucepan', and was suspended by the hook and chain.

LOWER DIVISION *(left)*,

Sundry round weights in black basalt (*nefritica*); marked in Roman figures.

74280 to 74290. Eleven round weights in bronze, marked with silver numerals, X, V, III, II, I, S or "*Semis*" (half), for the pounds, and :: ∴ : · S for fractions of pounds.

74308 to 74313. Six bronze WEIGHTS, in the shape of goats. These are marked P.X, P.V, P.III, P.II, P.I.

*74390 to 74393. Four large weights; a PIG, bearing the initials P.C (one hundred pounds); a CHEESE, and two huge KNUCKLE-BONES. (*Pompeii.*)

*Leaden weights, bearing the word "EME" on one side, and "HABEBIS" on the other—"*Buy, and you shall have.*" (*Pompeii.*)

74582 *et seq.* Measures for oil. (*Pompeii.*)

74599. Measure for liquids, of the weight of ten pounds.— The *Congius* spoken of by Pliny. (*Borgia.*)

*74600-1. Dry MEASURES. Their capacity was settled by the triangular crosspieces. Inscription: "D. D. P. P. HERC." (*Pompeii.*)

OUTSIDE THE WALL-CASE,

74602. Dry measure. (The wood is a restoration.) (*P.*)

WALL-CASES Nos. L. AND LI.,

Sundry kitchen utensils. (*Pompeii and Herculaneum.*)

MATHEMATICAL INSTRUMENTS.

TABLE-CASE No. LXI.,

*76657 to 76667. Plummets. (*Pompeii and Herculaneum.*)

*76670 *et seq.* Sundry pairs of compasses. (*P. and Herc.*)

*76684 Reducing compass. (*Pompeii.*)

†115630. CALLIPERS. This handsome specimen is exactly like the instrument used by modern sculptors. (1887, *P.*)

76689. Square. (*Pompeii.*)

*76690 *et seq.* Linear measures. (*Pompeii.*)

FISHING TACKLE.

76840 *et seq.* Netting needles. bronze and bone needles, quadruple fish-hook weighted.-Four hundred fish-hooks. (*P.*)
109703. A RUDDER, belonging probably to a bronze statue of "Abundance." (*Pompeii.*)
111845. Small iron ANCHOR; the only one yet found. (*P.*)

MUSICAL INSTRUMENTS.

TABLE-CASE No. LXII.,

*76945 *et seq.* SISTRA—jingling bronze rattles used in the worship of Isis. (*Pompeii.*)
*76942. CYMBALS of two kinds (Psalm. cl. 5). (*Pompeii.*)
111055. A bronze wind instrument, like an organ. It was fitted with a chain, apparently to be carried round the neck. (*Pompeii.*)
*76890. BAGPIPES found in the baaracks. The "dulci-mer" of Dan. iii. 5. Nero was fond of this instrument, and is said to have played it in public. It is the favourite instrument of the S. Italian peasantry. (*Pompeii.*)
*76891 *et seq.* FLAGEOLETS made of silver, bronze, and ivory. (*Pompeii.*)

TOYS, DICE, AND TICKTES FOR THEATRES.

TABLE-CASE No. LXIII.,

*76950 *et seq.* Knucklebones and dice; some constructed that they might be loaded. (*Pompeii.*)
*77087 *et seq.* Sundry checks or tickets (*tesserae*) for theatres and boxing matches, made of ivory. Observe the small numbered birds made of terra-cotta. These were checks for the upper row of seats, still called the "*piccio-naia*" or pigeon-loft, in Italy. (*P.* and *Herculaneum.*)
109880. Six nnmbered death's-heads (use unknown). (*P.*)

TOILET REQUISITES.

TABLE-CASE No. LXIII. *(bis)*,

77147 *et seq.* Bronze clasps (*fibulae*). (*P.* and *Herc.*)

77170. Fibula in the form of a horse.

114430. Bronze ring with the finger-bone of his owner.

77259 *et seq.* Bronze rings fitted with a small hey for jewel-cases. (*Pompeii.*)

77245. Sundry rings in bone and lead, bearing initials. (*Pompeii.*)

77174 *et seq.* Bronze bracelets, in the form of serpents, one with a silver medallion. (1863, *Pompeii.*)

*77213 *et seq.* Five perfect metal MIRRORS. One in a modern frame was found in the House of the Faun. (*P.*)

77291 *et seq.* These specimens have long been supposed to be perforated boxes for perfumes, made on the principle of the modern "*vinaigrette*"; but, in fact, they are cases for seals to be attached to parchments. The box contained the seal, and two or more threads of silk attached to the wax passed from the parchment through the holes. One of them may be seen represented upon the large fresco from the House of Pansa attached to the papyrus (see No.8598.p.2).

77298. Small rectangular bolts in ivory, for securing dressing-cases or small articles of furniture. (*Pompeii.*)

77318 *et seq.* Bone buttons and bronze studs. (*P.*)

77355 *et seq.* Ivory and bronze combs. (*Pompeii.*)

77363. BRONZE THIMBLE. (*Pompeii.*)

Small pots for cosmetics. (*Pompeii.*)

*77570. Pot of rock-crystal, still containing *rouge*. (*P.*)

Small flagons in alabaster and ivory, for perfumes. (*P.*)

SPINDLE, fitted with a bronze hook. (*Pompeii.*)

77518. Bronze winder, in nine divisions, for threads of different colour. (*Pompeii.*)

80088. Small toothed wheel, used as part of a bolt. (*P.*)

We draw attention to this little specimen to show how nearly the Romans had reached one of the leading principles of the modern clock.

Hairpins in bone and bronze, adorned with statuettes and busts; tooth-picks and earpickers. (*Pompeii* and *Herc.*)

WALL-CASES Nos. LII. AND LIII.,
Kitchen pots and pans. (*Pompeii* and *Herculaneum.*)

COLANDERS.

CASE LXIV., IN FRONT OF THE WINDOW.
Colanders perforated in graceful designs. (*P.* and *Herc.*)
77609. In the centre of this specimen a bas-relief of Venus with silver bracelets, holding out her hand to a small Cupid. (*Herculaneum.*)

NEAR THE BALUSTRADE OF THE MODEL OF POMPEII,
78579. Large CALDRON, nailed and bolted as our modern steam boilers. (*Pompeii.*)
78580. Large FIRE-PLUG, found in the palace of Tiberius at Capri. The rust of ages has sealed it hermetically.
This specimen once had water in it, which one could hear by shaking it. This has now completely evaporated.

78581. Bronze grating (*claustrum*), found before a window in Pompeii.

SURGICAL INSTRUMENTS (*Chirurgia.*)

TABLE-CASE LXV.,
Bistouries (surgical knives), spatulæ, sounds, and tweezers, some of which last belonged to lamps.
77738 *et seq.* "Directors."
77982. Curved dentated forceps, for removing foreign substances from cavities.

TABLE CASE LXVI.,
77986 *et seq* Fourteen bronze cupping vessels of modern shape, but ours are now made of glass.
78000-1. Spoons with head of a ram and of a woman.
78003. Lancet for bleeding.
78004. Silver spoon with elegant handle.
78005. Scissors with a spring, like shears.
78007. FLEAM for bleeding horses.

2

78008. TROCHAR for tapping for dropsy. A hole in the end gives an exit to the water.

78012. An ELEVATOR (or instrument for raising depressed portions of the skull) made of bronze.

*78026. A MALE CATHETER (aenea fistula).

*78027. A FEMALE CATHETER, 3 1/2 inches in length.

*78029. POMPEIAN FORCEPS, formed of two branches crossing, and working on a pivot. It was used for crushing small calculi.

*78030. SPECULUM UTERI. It is a tri-valvular dilator; the three valves, standing at right angles to the rest of the instrument, are jointly dependent on each other in the expansion transmitted only to one of them. When the three valves are in contact, the instrument for insertion is about an inch in circumference. By turning the screw, one valve is drawn nearer to the operator, and this forces the other two to open in a sidelong direction, producing thus a slow. regular, progressive dilatation, as extensive as may be required. The instrument can be held by the two curved handles in the left, while the right hand turns the screw. These movable handles are similar to those fitted to modern specula. (Pompeii.)

113264. SPECULUM UTERI. A quadrivalvular dilator of beautiful workmanship and very scientific costruction. (P.)

*78031. SPECULUM ANI. A bi-valvular dilator, probably used also for the uterus before the other one was known.

78032. Dentated forceps of elegant construction.

78121. Sound with flattened extremity, bifurcated for cutting the frenum of the tongue ; as used in modern surgery.

78034 et seq. Actual cauteries.

*78071. Surgical needle.

78137. Probes found in the cases to the left of them.

78195-6. Stones for sharpening instruments. (Stabiae.)

*78235. An INJECTION PROBE for females, with eight small holes arranged like wreaths.

*PILLS, SULPHUR, and other medicaments. (Stabiae.)

MORE SURGICAL INSTRUMENTS.

TABLE-CASE LXVI (bis),

On the 31.st of October 1887 the following items were found in a house at Pompeii which appears to have been the residence of a Medical man.

116437 et seq. Sundry forceps.

116460. Earthenware gallipot containing drugs, the nature of which is unknown.

116460 (bis). Plate with similar contents.

116438 Chemist's scales.

116439 et seq. Four square bronze weights. These have dots upon them to denote their value — no. 116443 weighs 14 grammes. Besides them are three weights of black stone (nefritica).

110088. Small bronze medicine spoon.

116459. Stone for instruments.

116456. Rusty scalpel.

116458. Iron spring scissors.

116450. Large bronze surgical needle.

116435. Uterine dilator similar to that in the preceding table-case.

116436. Anal dilator.

116451. Injecting probes.

116447. Bistouries.

116444. Bronze instrument case still containing its original instruments. — Sundry empty cases.

116441-2. Two inkstands in good preservation.

116453. The hinges and lock of the box which contained the above specimens.

IVORY ARTICLES (Miscellaneous.)

TABLE-CASES Nos. LXVII, LXVIII.,

78362 et seq. Fragments of furniture made of iron cased in ivory. — Ivory fragments from dressing-cases. — Bone spoons. (Pompeii.) •

110924. Statuette of Venus with dolphin. (*Pompeii.*)

78279. Statuette of boy wearing the "*bulla patricia.*" (*Pompeii.*)

78306. Fragments from the Curule chair. (*Pompeii.*)

109905 and -5 (*bis*). Two ivory panels (frame modern), carved on both sides, used as ornaments for furniture. (*P.*)

78288. Small bronze skeleton. (*Pompeii.*)

78289. Fine ivory death's-head.

IN THE WINDOW,

The skull and the right fore-arm are so small that they seem to have belonged to a young girl, who was probably a member of the family of Diomede at Pompeii. One of her teeth will be observed in perfect preservation. The various blocks of ashes collected in this case had surrounded the body, and still show the imprint of the breast, of the hands and fingers, as well as of the feet.

WRITING MATERIALS.

WALL-CASE No. LVI.,

Inkstands, pens, metal mirrors, serpentine bracelets. (*P.*)

75080. Inkstand still containing ink, *atramentum.* (*P.*)

†75091. Octagonal inkstand (found in a tomb at Terlizzi) of bronze, decorated in silver, with the seven divinities who presided over the seven days of the week,—namely, Apollo, Diana, Mars, Mercury, Jupiter, Venus and Saturn.

Martorelli, the archælogist (who wrote two volumes about this inkstand), thinks that it belonged to some astronomer of the time of Trajan.

110672. Bronze PEN, nibbed like a modern one. (*P.*)

IN A TUBE OF MODERN GLASS,

75095. Pen of reed, found in a papyrus at Herculaneum.

75099. Slabs of stone, which were covered with wax for writing upon with the "*stylus.*"

75113. Two bone "*styli.*" Pointed at one end and flat at the other, to rub out what one had written. (*Pompeii.*)

80111. Bracelet on the bone of a right arm. (*P.*)

75114. Bronze squares from the front of a strong box.

SADDLERY.

Wall-case (next the door) LVII.,

Cattle bells, harness, &c. Large number of bells for cattle. By pulling a wire in the side of this case, one of these bells is made to ring. (*Pompeii* and *Herculaneum.*)

74578. Small model of a biga, of very great interest, as showing us the form of Pompeian vehicles. (*Pompeii.*)

Harness for horses, consisting of scrolls, sprays, bits, nosebands, pole-heads, curb-chains, spurs, a stirrup (?), buckles, and other objects which can be readily identified.

75537. A fragment representing a blacksmith in the act of paring a hoof.

KITCHEN UTENSILS.

Wall-case LVIII,

Pastry moulds in the shape of shells. (*P.* and *H.*)

76352 *et seq.* Four shapes, representing a hare, a pig, a ham, and half a fowl. (*Pompeii.*)

76336. Implements for making pastry.—Pastry cutters.

76349. Cheese-graters.—Bronze kinives and spoons. (*P.*)

Wall-case LIX,

76543. Large egg frame, capable of cooking twenty-nine eggs at once. (*Inn, Pompeii.*)

76540-1. Very handsome andirons (?).

Tart dishes, frying-pans, gridirons, tongs, artistic fire-shovels, kitchen trivets. An iron trivet, much oxidised and covered with *lapilli*, with a pot firmly stuck to it by the oxidisation. — Seven spits.

Hanging up against the wall near the door,

78622. A bronze bell, shaped like a gong. (*Pompeii.*)

It has a beautiful tone, which may be heard by swinging the clapper which hangs before it.

THE COLLECTION OF GEMS.

(Oggetti preziosi.)

This collection has recently been scientifically arranged, and is divided into four principal sections, namely,—Gold Ornaments, Silver Plate, Engraved Gems, and Cameos.

The gold ornaments are very varied, and many of them are of extremely beautiful design. Some of them were found in Greek tombs in the South Italian provinces, but the majority are of the Roman period, and were discovered in the excavations at Pompeii.

The collection of Silver Plate is perhaps the most important extant, and shows a wonderful excellence of design and execution.

CAMEOS AND INTAGLIOS.

This collection consists of about a thousand specimens, many of which bear the name of Lorenzo de' Medici, and came from the Farnese collection. The ancient specimens are marked *"Ant.."* (Antique) and the mediæval ones *"xv."* (fifteenth century).

TAZZA FARNESE.

IN THE WINDOW,

*27611. .CUP OF ORIENTAL SARDONYX of inestimable merit and value, found either in the Castle of *Sant' Angelo* at Rome, or in Hadrian's villa at Tivoli. It came into the possession of Duke Charles of Bourbon when he was besieging Rome, and was already disfigured by a hole in the centre, which had been bored through it with the view, no doubt, of fixing it on a stand. It is the only known cameo of its size which has a composition engraved on both sides of it. On the outer side is a magnificent Medusa, and on the inner eight figures in relief representing Ptolemy Philadelphus consecrating the harvest festival instituted by Alexander the Great after the foundation of Alexandria. (*Ant.*)

FIRST TABLE.—FIRST COMPARTMENT (*next window.*)
25833 to 25899. (*Note especially.*)

1. *Onyx*. THE EDUCATION OF BACCHUS. The infant god, mounted on a lion led by a nymph, is held up by one of the *Nysiades*; behind, *Nysa* seated. *Ant.*

5. *Onyx*. NEPTUNE and PALLAS disputing about the name to be given to a rising city. Inscribed HY—probably meaning *Pyrgotele*. *Ant.*

*6. *Onyx*. DÆDALUS and ICARUS. Two females admiring the prodigy—probably Pasiphae and Diana Dictyna—personifying fhe Cretan City. XV.

8. *Oriental Onyx*. TRIUMPH of BACCHUS and SILENUS. The car is drawn by two Psyches, the reins held by Cupid, while another pushes the car. *Ant.*

*16. *Onyx*. JUPITER overwhelming the Titans. Legend, ΑΘΗΝΙΩΝ. *Ant.*

17. *Onyx*. COCK-FIGHT, in presence of two Cupids, one lamenting his defeat, the other victorious. *Ant.*

19. *Sardonyx*. HEAD of OMPHALE. *Ant.*

25. *Sardonyx*. HOMER; name on the mantle. *Ant.*

*30. *Agate*. JUPITER SERAPIS, in high-relief. *Ant.*

*32. *Agate*. Head of MEDUSA. *Ant.*

38. *Agate*. OTHRYADES dying. *Ant.*

†41. *Sardonyx*. SATYR dancing. A fragment. *Ant.*

†44. *Sardonyx*. AUGUSTUS. Attributed to *Dioscorides*.

†47. *Onyx*. AURORA in her chariot. *Ant.*

*48. *Oriental Onyx*. A FAUN carrying the infant Bacchus.

52. *Onyx*. A fine head, perhaps CICERO. *Ant.*

55. *Oriental Onyx*. VENUS and CUPID.

†57. *Sardonyx*. CENTAUR. *Ant.*

*60. *Oriental Onyx.* SCULPTOR chisselling a vase. *Ant.*

*65. *Agate.* DIRCE'S PUNISHMENT. Fragment.

1857. *Onyx enammelled.* VESTAL , a superb head. *Ant·*

SECOND COMPARTMENT.

25900 to 26042.

69. *Agate.* Ariobarzanus III.. king of Cappadocia (?). *Ant.*

77. *Sardonyx.* DOMITIAN. Laurel crowned. XV.

86. *Onyx.* HERCULES strangling the serpents. *Ant.*

90. *Sapphire.* Veiled head of LIVIA. XV.

93. *Emerald.* Lotus-crowned head of ISIS. *Ant.*

99. *Lapis-lazuli.* Tiberius crowned with laurel. XV.

105. *Emerald.* Bust of JUPITER SERAPIS. *Ant.*

123. *Jacinth.* CLEOPATRA. XV.

124. *Onyx.* MARSYAS bound and MERCURY. *Ant.*

134. *Onyx.* Leda and the swan. *Ant.*

147. *Sardonyx.* HERCULES and the lion. XV.

154. *Onyx.* GANYMEDE AND THE EAGLE. XV.

167. *Garnet.* SAMSON, with legend. XV.

171. *Agate.* DOMITIAN. XV.

†188. *Sardonyx.* AURORA on a *quadriga.* *Ant.*

The artist adapted the different strata of the stone to give each horse a distinct colour. According to Winckelmann, their colours indicate dawn, day, twilight, and night.

193. *Onyx.* CUPID; legend—ΦΙΛΩ, *I love. Ant.*

197. *Onyx.* Hand pulling an ear; MNHMONEYE, *remember. Ant.*

198. *Onyx.* Hand-in-hand, OMONOIA—*concord. Ant.*

201. *Onyx.* GANYMEDE horne by the eagle. *Ant.*

†203. *Agate.* THETIS on a dolphin , with Triton and Zephyr. XV.

206. *Glass.* Tiberius. (*Pompeii.*)

INTAGLIOS.

SECOND TABLE — FIRST COMPARTMENT.
26043 to 26209.

*209. *Carnelian.* AJAX and Cassandra at the Palladium. *A.*

†214. *Chrysolite.* PALLAS: XV.

†215. *Chalcedony.* ANTONINUS PIUS (?). XV.

221. *Carnelian.* SOLON. Legend,—ΣΟΛΩΝΟΣ. *Ant.*

228. *Amethyst.* IOLE ; a fine head. XV.

230. *Sapphire.* Fine bust of JUNO. *Ant.*

∴ 231. *Carnelian.* Head of MARCUS AURELIUS. *Ant.*

*232. *Amethyst.* DIANA with ΑΠΟΛΛΩΝΙΟΣ inscribed in Greek. A gem of great celebrity. *Ant.*

†234. *Calcedony.* ACTOR with a mask. XV.

244. *Beryl.* Head of SERGIUS GALBA. XV.

248. *Carnelian.* THE CAR OF THE SUN. *Ant.*

250. *Amethyst.* ANTONINUS PIUS. *Ant.*

253. *Amethyst.* THETIS on two sea-horses. *Ant.*

254. *Carnelian.* PERSEUS with Medusa's head. Inscribed *"Dioscorides."* *Ant.*

256. *Carnelian.* HADRIAN, crowned. *Ant.*

268. *Carnelian.* Fine head of PLATO. XV.

276. *Carnelian.* JULIUS CÆSAR. XV.

287. *Garnet.* Bust of CLEOPATRA. *Ant.*

Carnelian. (The *first* stone from the left , without a number). Handsome bust of JUNO. (*Pompeii.*)

329. *Sardonyx.* MARS crowned by Victory. *Ant.*

SECOND COMPARTMENT.
26210 to 26389.

†390. *Carnelian.* SACRIFICE. Group of 18 figures. XV.

408. *Carnelian.* SILENUS upon an ass. Group. XV.

413: *Carnelian.* PESCENNIUS. Inscribed *"Pescennio".* XV.

417. *Sanguine Jasper.* SACRIFICE. XV.

419. *Carnelian.* LIVIA and TIBERIUS. Group. XV.

439. *Carnelian.* Strength conquered by Beauty.

455. *Sardonyx.* CUPID dedicating one wing to the Sun. XV.
473. *Chalcedony.* AFRICA PERSONIFIED. Engraved with unintelligible characters. *Ant.*

OTHER INTAGLIOS AND CAMEOS.

·THIRD TABLE—FIRST COMPARTMENT.
26390 to 26766.

Intaglios of less importance.

SECOND COMPARTMENT.
26767 to 26965.

(CAMEOS).

961. *Agate.* MINERVA, fully armed. Bust. XV.
967. *Onyx.* AURORA in her chariot. *Ant.*
988. *Onyx.* THE THREE GRACES. XV.
1003. *Onyx.* MINERVA. XV.
†1021. *Lapis-lazuli.* MINERVA armed. XV.
†1024. *Onyx.* ALEXANDER THE GREAT. XV.
1044. *Onyx.* MÆCENAS (?). XV.
1046. *Agate.* SOCRATES. XV.

FOURTH TABLE—FIRST COMPARTMENT.
26966 to 27123.

1162. *Agate.* Head of Cicero, KI-KE-PO. *Ant.*
A necklace of scarabs.

SECOND COMPARTMENT.
27124 to 27348.

1375. *Green Jasp.* Aurora. XV.
†1352. A *bulla* mounted with gold wire, representing a man and his wife. Some think that this a portrait of Marcus Aurelius and Faustina. *Ant.*

FIFTH TABLE.
27349 to 27610.

Many portraits in intaglio.

1520. *Sardonyx*. Jupiter. Bust. xv.

1540. *Sea-shell*. Three Cupids drawing water. xv.

1701 *et seq*. *Agates*. Perfume vases. *Ant.*

Agate. A knuckle-bone. *Ant.*

Large silver-gilt rings belonging to Cardinal Farnese. Some similar rings are exhibited in the Musee Cluny at Paris.

LAST TABLE.

One hundred and forty intaglios and stone all from recent excavations at Pompeii. Observe especially the numbers 27651,-27665,-27653,-14565,-14566,-27617,-114562, and in the last row a beautiful glass intaglio (n.° 109579) representing a Minerva standing.

SILVER.

In an upright glass case :

CUPS AND VASES.

TOP SHELF,

25289. Silver PAIL with bronze handle decorated with a bas-relief of a lady at her bath. (*Herculaneum.*)

25376-77-80-81. Four BACCHIC CUPS executed in magnificent high—relief, representing Centaurs and Genii. (*P.*)

15367. CUP representing in bas-relief Minerva in a chariot drawn by two horses. (*Pompeii.*)

25565. Fragment of a cup representing chariots driven by children. (*Herculaneum.*)

25301. Mortar representing the Apotheosis of Homer. One of the most famous specimens of ancient silver work. In the centre is the poet draped and veiled , borne heavenwards by an eagle. On the right a female figure representing the Odyssey. On the left is the Iliad personified armed cap-à-pic. (*Herculaneum.*)

25681. CUP adorned with Bacchic figures.

111149. MORTAR adorned with bas-relief representing

Theseus fighting against one of the Amazones on horseback
(*Pompeii.*)

SECOND SHELF,

25284-5-8. Three BOWLS on tripod stands of Renaissance
work. (*Rome.*)
25343. CENSER with cover and chains. (*Herculaneum.*)
3571o. Two SYSTRA. A musical instrument. (*Pompeii.*)
25722 and 110841. Two BOTTLES for liquids: one with
chains. (*Pompeii.*)

THIRD SHELF,

25691 *el seq.* Six pitchers. (*Pompeii and Herculaneum.*)
111768-9. Two large pitchers with two handles. Each
weighs about 10 lbs. (*Herculaneum.*)

GOLD ORNAMENTS.

(*Greek and Etruscan.*)

FIRST DIVISION *(on the left)*,

†25234 *et seq.* A pair of very large earrings of pyramidal
shape.—A ring, with an agate intaglio representing an
Amazon and a small gold coin of Syracuse representing a
portrait of a woman. (Gift of Baron d'Arbou Castillon 1864
found in a tomb at Taranto).
24852. GOLD BULL with Phœnician and Greek inscription.
(*Syracuse.*)
24826. KID in massive gold from Edessa in Mesopotamia.
(*Borgia Collection.*)
24876-8. Two perfume vases in blue glass mounted on
a gold stand. (*Venosa.*)
Ten necklaces. The following are the most remarkable:—
*24883. Splendid necklace formed of twenty-one Silenus
masks and fifty-eight acorns and *fleurs-de-lys.* (*Armento.*)
*24858. NECKLACE OF LACE-WORK, with elegantly woven
pendants.
42.9 27Necklace consisting of seven gold parallelograms.

24862. Necklace with blue beads threaded upon it, to which are attached nineteen masks of Jove, Medusa, and Silenus. (*Chiusi.*)

24887. Necklace of a gold chain with garnets. In the centre a small octagonal column of garnet. (*Sant'Agata dei Goti.*)

BETWEEN THE NECKLACES,

24893. GOLD TIARA formed of a curved spray with leaves and flowers set with garnets, and small gold butterflies. (*Fasano.*)

24854-5-6. Three specimens of beautiful workmanship representing cornucopiae with lions' heads. These are thought to have been earrings. (*Capua.*)

Below them, a pair of earrings in the shape of butterflies.

Among fourteen rings, observe a ring 25157 set with an emerald plasma which is thought to have contained poison. (*Ruvo.*)

24844. Fillet, with a head of Medusa, in relief. (*Toro.*)

*24865 *et seq.* NINE BROOCHES (*fibulae*), artistically wrought in filagree, ending in the head of a ram in Etruscan Style.

(*Roman Period.*).

25000. LARGE GOLD LAMP, weighing nearly two pounds, and having its handle formed of a leaf. It is the only gold lamp yet found in Pompeii. (Grammes 896).

EARRINGS.

SECOND WALL (*first and second divisions*),

*Two hundred and fifty two gold earrings, of which hundred and two are in the shape of a segment of an apple, and many are drops with a pearl as a pendant; seventeen represent genii, two are of the shape of almonds, and others are set with emeralds. (*Pompeii* and *Herculaneum.*)

RINGS.

Three hundred and twenty-three gold rings, most of them set with fine stones.

The first five rows consist of rings from Pompeii, and the last two rows of rings from Herculaneum.—Note ;

†In the second row a ring 25181 bearing a mask engraved on carnelian, which was found at Pompeii by King Charles III, who wore it for many years. When this King inherited the throne of Spain, he handed over the ring to the Museum.

24732-3-4. Three rings with the finger-bones of their owners. (*Pompeii.*)

The *provenance* of the rings in the next compartment is unknown, with a few unimportant exceptions which came from the Campanian provinces.

Among them will be found—

A very large ring of unusual shape, with fragment of glazing. Thought to have been a perfume ring. (*Herc.*)

24902. Gold ring. Man and woman shaking hands. Probably an engagement ring. (*Ponza*).

25085. Very large head of Brutus engraved on gold, grammes 3,50. (*S. Maria di Capua*). Inscribed "ΑΝΑΞΙΛΑΣ ΕΠΟΕΙ ".

The last row consists of rings of the fifteenth century. Note high-relief of woman in onyx.

NECKLACES.

Third division,

Thirty-two necklaces. Note especially ;

111114. Two vine-leaf necklaces, one of forty-eight and the other of forty-six leaves. (*Pompeii.*)

†113576. REMARKABLE NECKLACE of ribbon wire set with eight large pearls and nine emeralds. At one end of it is a gold disc set with an emerald, at the other end is a hook. This is one of the richest necklaces of antiquity. (Length 315 millimetres). (*Found near Pompeii*, 1884).

24650. BULLÆ PATRICIÆ. These trinkets were worn round the necks of patrician boys in Roman times, and were dedicated to the gods when the boys arrived at man's estate. They were called "*bullæ*" (bubbles) from their shape, and are represented on the statues of boys of noble birth. (*Herculaneum.*)

25260. LONG GOLD CHAIN, beautifully worked. This chain was found, together with several of the gold ornaments already described, on the first floor of a house at Pompeii, where eleven persons (whose skeletons were found) had taken refuge. (Length, 2 3/4 yards).

24845-6. Two handsome brooches, to which two gold pomegranates have been suspended.

24857. LION and SPHINX brooch. (*Herculaneum.*)

25222-3. In the flat case are two remarkable buttons with seated female figures in red enamel. (*Pompeii.*)

BRACELETS.

FOURTH DIVISION,

Eighty-one bracelets of various kinds.

*24825. Two large serpeatine bracelets, weighing two pounds (the largest yet found). (*House of the Faun, P.*)

109587. BRACELET of gold wire twisted into figures of 8. (*Pompeii.*)

*24842. BRACELET of two cornucopiæ wiih lions' heads. (*Herculaneum.*)

The flat portion of this case contains some gold leaf, a purse made of gold network, lady's hair-net of gold wire in perfect preservation, fillets in gold braid.

ROCK CRYSTAL, AMBER.

FIFTH DIVISION,

Many fragments of rock crystal representing insects, cups, a spoon, &c. Several agate scent bottles. (*Pompeii.*)

†27613. A CIRCULAR PIECE OF GLASS, usually called a magnifying lens. This unique specimen has given rise to much discussion. (*Pompeii.*)

Several fragments of amber, among them a small statuette

(25813) of a man wearing a wig, and wrapped in a mantle. (*Pompeii.*)

The rest of the amber was found at *Ruvo.*

25810. A cock and a parrot in mother-of-pearl.

OTHERS OBJECTS IN SILVER.

LEFT CORNER,—WALL-CASE, NEAR THE WINDOW,

A box containing fragments of silver from furniture decorations; much oxydised and mingled with lapilli. (*P.*)

Silver crescent, tweezers and clasps. (*Pompeii.*)

Bracelets, brooches, rings, necklace, and two strigils hung on a ring.

RIGHT CORNER,—WALL-CASE, NEAR THE WINDOW,

Many cups with saucers, in very good preservation. (*P.*)

NEXT WALL,

25695. Silver trays, one oblong, the others round. (*H.*)

WALL-CASE BEYOND THE DOOR *(hanging from top shelf),*

25494. BRONZE SUN-DIAL faced with silver, in the shape of a ham. The hours are indicated by radiating lines, across which run irregular horizontal lines. Below these are the names of the months. The tail served as a gnomon. (*Herculaneum.*)

25496. Beneath the dial two delicate silver colanders are suspended. (*Herculaneum.*)

CUPS.

Twenty eight cups, among which, two chased cups.

25372. Handsome vase with spiral ornament surmounted with the head of a woman with her hair dressed in modern style.

Pastry-mould in the shape of a shell.

Spoons of various shapes. (*Pompeii* and *Herculaneum.*)

Small spoons with pointed ends, which are thought to have served as forks. (*Pompeii* and *Herculaneum.*)

Sixteen saucepans, the handles engraved with designs. Sauce-ladles. (*Pompeii* and *Herculaneum.*)

LAST WALL-CASE *(top shelf)*,

Several cups adorned with exquisite foliage. Observe; *25287. BACCHIC CUP, worked in bas-relief of ivy.

25300. Mortar-shaped cup adorned with beautiful leaves and sprays. (*Pompeii.*)

25495. Satyr seated on a rock playing the lyre before a hermes. (*Herculaneum.*)

109688. Diminutive skeleton very well executed. (*P.*)

†25490. THE DEATH OF CLEOPATRA. A very fine bas-relief on the reverse of a circular mirror. (*Herculaneum.*)

25489. ABUNDANCE. Circular *plaque*, of perfect preservation. (*Pompeii.*)

109331. Male figure seated beneath a tree. (*Herc.*)

25492-3. DIANA AND APOLLO. Two medallions in high-relief.

25699. A man and a woman conversing. Silver inlaid on copper. (*Herculaneum.*)

25482-3. Two arms well moulded, belonging probably to a statuette.

25497-8. Two hairpins, one representing Venus and Cupid, the other Venus and Adonis. (*Pompeii.*)

www.ingramcontent.com/pod-product-compliance
Lightning Source LLC
Chambersburg PA
CBHW021526270326
41930CB00008B/1120